From Out of the Blue
A Spiritual Adventure

Steve Travis

1469 Morstein Road
West Chester, Pennsylvania 19380 USA

For my parents, Anne and Steve
For Anne Marie, Cathy, and Mark
For my grandparents, Louise and Dominick
To those who search, and
To Shirley MacLaine, for helping to open the door.

From Out of the Blue: A Spiritual Adventure
by Steve Travis

Copyright © 1990 by Steve Travis

Cover design by Bob Boeberitz. Cover photograph of figure by Peter Gowland. Cover photograph of sky by Craig Olsen.

Library of Congress Card Number: 90-070477
International Standard Book Number: 0-924608-05-6

Manufactured in the United States of America.

Scriptures quoted throughout this text are taken from The New American Standard Bible © THE LOCKMAN FOUNDATION 1960, 1962, 1963, 1968, 1971, 1972, 1973, 1975, 1977.

Published by Whitford Press
a division of
Schiffer Publishing, Ltd.
1469 Morstein Road
West Chester, Pennsylvania 19380
Please write for a free catalog.
This book may be purchased from the publisher.
Please include $2.00 postage.
Try your bookstore first.

Contents

Acknowledgements

I would like to thank Santi for his love, enthusiasm, encouragement, the bejeweled book meditation, and for introducing me to rebirthing; Verna Yater for the dream work, her breakthrough workshops, and her commitment to vision; Elwood Babbitt, Kevin Ryerson, Verna Yater, and their spirit guides Dr. Fisher, Tom McPherson, and Indira Latari, respectively, for their spiritual offerings; Stephen Laberge for his revolutionary lucid dream work; Jim Leonard, Phil Lout, Sondra Ray, and Leonard Orr for their rebirthing material; Stephen Arroyo, Liz Greene, Jeff Green, and Martin Schulman for their spiritual and karmic astrology; Robert Monroe for his out-of-body material; Astrologers Dave Lajala and Marion Stoneman for their knowledge and insights; Sondra Ray for her affirmations material; Nora Grafton for her inspiring definition of the word "spiritual"; Jeff Brouws for his photograph; Sandra Griffin for lending me extremely inaccessible taped material; Mark Tidd for his generosity (without which this book may not sanely have been written); and Ellen Sue Taylor, Tim Scott, and everyone at Schiffer Publishing and the Whitford Press division for sharing the vision.

Preface

This book can be used in a number of ways. It can be enjoyed purely as an adventure in consciousness. It can be used experientally by consulting the appendices. The bibliography is set up as a recommended reading section according to category.

In some instances I've changed the order of events, but everything you are about to read actually happened to me.

In his wonderfully inspiring *Illusions: The Adventures of a Reluctant Messiah*, Richard Bach writes, "Here is a test to find whether your mission on earth is finished: if you're alive, it isn't."

While I share much of what I have learned since embarking on the spiritual path in this book, I'm still here.

This is my story.

Introduction

I'd like to begin this adventure by clarifying my definitions of a few important words that will be used throughout the text.

I will be using the words God, all that is, and the universe interchangeably, because it is my belief that they are all the same.

If the word "he" appears as a pronown to signify people in general, it is meant to include both sexes, and is being used for the sake of simplicity.

Since this book is subtitled "*A Spiritual Adventure*, I think it fitting to talk a little about the word "spiritual." Many people have their own definitions of the word. Some even confusing it with the word "religious."

Having found some definitions that fit mine while reading Nora Grafton's lively and inspirational *My Own True Psychic Adventures*, I'd like to quote from that book. Ms. Grafton wisely differentiates the word "religious" from "spiritual."

> By "religion" I mean...church doctrines, dogmas and rituals...a state of loyalty to, and practice of certain tenets of their chosen denomination or church which are governed by canon law, and therefore limited, or restricted.
>
> To be spiritual is to be free in one's choice of expression, to be able to soar in consciousness to great heights; it is to seek to recover from the soul's inner awareness, its abundant knowledge of Universal Truths...to know love, and to express love; to have compassion, because these spiritual ones walk, by choice, along a path that is illumined for them by the Light of God's...Love, and they allow themselves to be guided

by His...Wisdom. And as they grow...in their awareness of Truth in Its limitless universality, reaching for their soul's at-one-ment with Deity, the veils are parted and much of great wonder is revealed to them, and...their lives become filled with marvelous spiritual gifts that result in experiences so astounding that men speak of them as "miracles."

'And it shall be in the last days,'
saith God,
I will pour forth of My
Spirit upon all flesh;
And your sons and your daughters
shall prophesy,
And your young men shall see visions,
And your old men shall dream dreams;'

--Acts 2:17

Part I

From Out of the Blue

Chaos breeds possibility.

Chapter 1

Existentialism and Metaphysics

It was September. The year is unimportant, for the experiences are timeless.

To be honest with you, I wasn't really looking for anything. Well, *almost* anything. I was looking for a book--any book. I was between projects, waiting for the next one to begin, and I was bored. I already had played for a week or two; and while playing in the beautiful Southern Californian town of Santa Barbara was one of life's easier pleasures, I now was bored.

Eight months earlier, in January, I had found myself in a similar predicament. I ended up with a book snatched off a friend's bookshelf that dealt with leaving one's body. I always had wanted to read about that sort of thing, if merely for the sake of fascination.

A number of friends and acquaintances had reported their out-of-body experiences to me. I listened to their stories with much interest, but I of course dismissed them with a mixture of disbelief and envy.

When I got home that night, I quickly read the back cover and the table of contents of the book on out-of-body experiences, and then tossed it aside. It looked sort of interesting, but I wanted something else--perhaps something more real.

This time I went to the bookcase of a roommate who was in the process of moving out. His library was comprised primarily of film books. Among them were three books written by Shirley MacLaine. I assumed that they were all autobiographies of the Hollywood variety. On impulse I scooped up all three. One of these would be lightweight enough to end my boredom.

Unknowingly, I scanned the blurbs on each book in their chronological order. The first in this trilogy dealt with MacLaine's acting career. I was right, Hollywood fluff. The second one apparently had to do with a trip MacLaine had taken to China. I had vaguely remembered reading about this in the papers years ago. But the third book, *Out on a Limb*, looked the most provocative. The front-cover photographer had caught an extremely sober-looking MacLaine staring point-blank into the lens, with a foreboding burnt-orange horizon behind her. I had no idea what lay within.

With the search for an interesting book ended, I began reading. Unfortunately, after a chapter or so, MacLaine kept me stranded on the beach in Malibu a little too long, causing me to dry-dock the book on my dresser.

My life at the time proceeded at a rather quick pace. I remember going out a lot with people with whom I worked. We'd go dancing. We'd drink a little.

I was leading--for me--a routine life: working for a major utility by day, partying by night. I wrote songs in my free time, a pattern that began twenty years previous. I had just turned 31.

My nights would end routinely, too. I would put some pocket change in my top dresser drawer and find MacLaine staring up at me from the cover of her abandoned book through the accumulating dust. (Now I knew why they were called "dust covers.") I remember coming in slightly bombed some nights and downright laughing at her, "So austere Shirl, what is your problem?" This was a few years before the media started taking potshots at her for her metaphysical beliefs.

Yet even while mocking her, I never thought to return the book to its proper shelf. She sat night after night, like some sort of literary lady in waiting. That it was for me she persevered, I had no idea.

By spring my temporary stint with the utility company ended and I was forced to look for some new means of support. I quickly found some consulting work that would effortlessly coast me through the summer. Working a six-hour day coincided neatly with the season.

Life was sweet. I was tan. I had a brief end-of-summer fling. Then I was back in between projects again.

Now this sort of life might seem rather fast or temporal to some, but I wasn't looking to live this way forever. I was attempting to live out the existential quest as much as possible while working in the economical structure of the 1980s.

I wanted to make enough money so that I could afford to make some demos (demonstration tapes) of some songs I had written. I sincerely wanted to get my songs published. Then I would have enough money to be able to pursue my existential quest.

My main goal was to be able to be subsidized by some creative act that I was good at, enjoyed doing, and that would yield big rewards. This could support me in traveling (something I still hadn't done enough of), in writing or anything that communicated my ideas to large groups of people in a positive way, and in pursuing other time-consuming artistic interests.

Working 40 hours a week at some boring, repetitive job that I just happened to be good at--in this case telemarketing--was nonsense. There *had* to be more, and in my art I would find it. But in the meantime, I was living a quiet rebellion.

So there I was, not looking for anything--at least not on a conscious level--in Santa Barbara, bored on a sunny September afternoon in my living room.

On this particular day I was feeling especially antsy. I quickly scanned *TV Guide*. Nothing. I did the crossword puzzle. Then from out of the blue something popped into my consciousness. I remembered the MacLaine book, buried beneath bills and dust in my dresser. Without a second thought I dashed through the dining room to my bedroom, grabbed the book, whizzed back through to the living room, and landed somewhere between the chair and the ottoman on which I had been sitting.

Slightly out of breath, I sat and scanned through the book. Having remembered my experience with it previously, I knew it was a long shot. But I was bored. Besides, I was in a frivolous state of mind. Reading about someone else's life, especially someone whom I dubbed "fun" as I imagined MacLaine to be from her screen appearances, would be cotton candy for the mind.

So I started the book again from the beginning, but with one very major difference. I couldn't put it down!

This was not empty calories, like the sugar I was expecting. This was philosophical debate on a metaphysical scale. This was somebody with intelligence, someone whose thinking process mirrored my own. Also like me she tended to give people the impression of not being very well-grounded, of being more "out there" than "in there" at times. Yet she like me was someone whose questioning nature upset these very people.

This was someone who persevered with the tough questions regardless of public opinion. Guts in intellect. I respected her.

The metaphysical debate in the book lay shrouded under the auspices of a whirlwind romance MacLaine was having with a British diplomat. I reacted querulously to this portion of the book, wondering where it all was leading.

But after the actress returned from Sweden to her beachfront apartment in Malibu this query was cleared up, and the book swiftly and ingeniously became detective mystery-meets-science fiction with spiritual implications.

After reading the MacLaine book, I wanted to know more. I had to know more! I wanted proof. Her book contained information on reincarnation, trance channel mediums, UFOs, and out-of-body experiences. In some crazy mixed-up way these all somehow were connected. But before I subscribed to these seemingly cosmic comic-book beliefs, I needed my own experience of them.

I didn't know where to begin. My head was filled with a million questions, and I knew no one with the answers.

It was mentioned in the MacLaine book that Kevin Ryerson, the trance channel medium whom MacLaine invited to her Malibu home for a reading, lived in Santa Barbara. This was a lead, but it proved to be a fast dead end. By the time the book was published, he had moved away to Northern California.

I started doing little things, like reading various passages out of the Bible, looking up words like "spirit" in the dictionary for precise definitions, and researching parts of the book I had questioned. It was exciting. I had the definite feeling that I was on to something. Yet nothing really had happened.

Chapter 2

Blithe Spirits

I knew I needed to read more. There was a whole world of meta-physical books just waiting to be devoured, and I didn't have to go too far out of my way to find this material, either. On my table top in my bedroom, I discovered Robert Monroe's *Journeys Out of the Body* under a quiet layer of dust. I had flippantly tossed it aside at the beginning of the year.

It was interesting to me how this particular book picked up where the MacLaine book left off, and how eight months previous I had started and stopped reading them both on the same day, only to find myself now reading them both with great interest.

Through the MacLaine book and later in a psychic development class, I had learned that there were no such things as coincidences. But at the time I began experiencing this phenomenon I just called it "strange."

I shook off this strangeness matter-of-factly and began reading the Monroe book. But I was impatient. I was dying to have an out-of-body experience. Enough of all this reading. Out of my anxiousness to get to the guts, the "how to" part of the book, I quickly followed the table of contents to that very chapter. The technique seemed simple enough. That night I attempted one such journey.

One needed to begin by laying in a comfortable environment. I opted for my bed. With eyes closed you were to visualize a point in space about a foot away from your forehead with focused concentration. As I did this I quickly lost conception of time.

I then saw swirling energy patterns out of each eye, as I continued to hold my concentration. They looked like the swirls an electric mixer makes in cake batter. I saw these two identical designs as white static electricity on a black spatial background.

I could feel that I was getting extremely close to leaving my body --or having some other new experience, and I got scared. Having been raised Catholic, a belief system I no longer subscribed to, the fear that swept through me was of being possessed. If I were to succeed in leaving my body, would it not then be vacant for some other entity to occupy?

MacLaine had not mentioned this possibility in her book when she spoke of her out-of-body experience, or if she had, I had not remembered it. If Monroe had mentioned it in his book, I had not yet reached that section, as I had skipped to the "how to" section in my haste.

I suspect that there was a part of me of which I then was unaware that doubted that I would be lucky enough actually to have this experience.

In my panic I quickly snapped myself out of this trance. I lay with heart thumping and curled for comfort in the fetal position. When I was relaxed enough, I allowed myself to fall asleep.

The next day I was angry at myself for not following through. I had come so close, which I really didn't expect, and I blew it. I supposed that in the safety of daylight it was easy for me to feel this way. Nonetheless, I was angry, and for another reason, too. Would I have this chance again? If so, how long would I have to wait?

I worked on my fear the entire next day. I affirmed that possession would not take place. While I no longer considered myself Catholic, there were some aspects of that faith that I did hold on to, and prayer was one of them. So I prayed that I would be protected and that if I was meant to have this experience I would.

By late afternoon I was feeling confident. I couldn't wait for night to come so that I again could journey outward. I suppose that it's possible to practice the technique in the daytime, but with the brightness outside and the noise factor involved, it hadn't occurred to me to do so. I still was waiting to hear when work would begin on a new project I had been offered, so sleeping in the middle of the day didn't fit into my lifestyle anyway.

That night I again followed the instructions from the Monroe book. This time I genuinely was not afraid. I experienced a similar version of the swirling electrical static patterns, and I then was out of my body. I didn't recall actually leaving my body--if that is in fact what occurred.

I think the reason I didn't actually remember leaving my body or floating just under the ceiling and looking down at my physical body asleep in bed, as many people report, was because it would have been too much for me. Yes, I had worked on my fear of possession, and yes, I did very much want to experience this supernatural phenomenon, but fear of the unknown still loomed within me.

I remember standing next to my bed in what felt like a dream. I looked over at my guitar amplifier. There was a television set superimposed over it. This was odd. It was then that I realized that I must have left my body.

I was excited! Always seeking proof and now knowing that I was on some other plane that had possibly bled through to the physical, I wanted to see how I looked. So I attempted to walk over to my full-length mirror. It was like walking waist deep through gelatin. I walked in a floating manner, similar to the way the astronauts walked on the moon.

But before I had a chance to look into the mirror, when I finally arrived at that part of the room, I experienced what I at first thought were energy patterns. Upon closer inspection through the use of my eyes and senses, it appeared that these energy patterns actually were spirit entities!

To my left there were two female entities and to my right one male. All three of them were very short, probably just under five feet in height. The reason they had caught my attention in the first place was because they were laughing at me!

I wasn't exactly in the frame of mind to attempt conversation with these beings and find out what the joke was. I was petrified!

Before they could collectively shout "boo!", I jumped back into my physical body, which was asleep on the other side of the room. I woke with a jolt.

When I woke the next morning, I didn't immediately remember the chilling episode. I usually needed something in the course of the day to trigger my memory of events that took place in the dream state. There are techniques available for remembering one's dreams. Unfortunately, however, these techniques were not made available to me at this time.

I don't remember what it was that triggered my memory later that day, but when I did gain recall of the episode, I convinced myself that it was just a dream. The television set that was superimposed over my guitar amplifier was the main cause of my concern. If this truly was an out-of-body experience, why was anything in my room altered?

I continued reading the Monroe book. I had skipped to the "how to" section of the book so that I could begin my experimentation. Now I read the book from the beginning. What captured my interest here had to do with some explanation of the astral plane. This plane, it was explained, was populated with entities who had just recently crossed over to the other side, and with those who were between planes. Many of these entities did not know--or did not want to believe--that they were in fact dead. I imagined that many of them had no belief system or one that was not strong enough at the time of their transitions to propel them to other planes. Or maybe the prospect of being dead was too shocking for them to assimilate.

It was further explained that in this aspect of the spirit dimension, reality was manufactured by one's thoughts. Since there obviously was no physical body to lug around, everything was communicated and formed by the thought processes.

It was explained that many of the objects to be found on this plane were common objects from the material plane, such as televisions and automobiles. *Televisions*? I imagined that having these sort of objects around was comforting to entities unaware of their true states, and that in their frenzy to come to terms with their new environments they unintentionally created these objects.

I again found it strange that I read about this "manufacturing reality by thought" concept on the astral plane the very day after my evening encounter with the entities and the superimposed television. Quite frankly, I was amazed.

Then something came into my consciousness. When I thought about it, I couldn't remember ever having a dream that took place in my bedroom. As an adult I would have dreams that took place in the bedroom of my youth, but never in the bedroom that I occupied at the time of the dream. So I now was entertaining the possibility that I may have left my body the previous night and that I actually did encounter three entities on the astral plane.

Feeling energized after reading *Out on a Limb*, I spoke of the book to almost every human that crossed my path. I recommended it to friends and family, my roommates, and even to people I met by chance. One of the people I mentioned it to was my landlady.

The roommate who had invited me to move into the house had been a friend of this woman and her brother since they all were in their teens. This same roommate also was indirectly responsible for my reading the MacLaine book because it was from his library that I had pulled the book.

Linda was a few years older than me, and due to the friendship she had with my roommate, Tim, the tenant-landlady relationship was pretty casual. She would come over once in a while. Occasionally we would go out socially as a group. I felt especially comfortable in sharing some of the information from the MacLaine book with her. While she had not read the book, she certainly was open to its possibilities. Since she was so receptive and because it was her house in which I had had my experience, I was prompted to tell her of my alleged out-of-body exploit.

Her dark eyes grew large as I concluded my adventure--and for good reason. The house was bequeathed to Linda and her brother, she explained, by her grandparents. They had built it in the 1920s. My bedroom had been the master bedroom. This was where Linda's grandparents slept.

Linda's mother, an only child, occupied one of the other two bedrooms. Her mother, she added, died at age 26, shortly after Linda was born. Her grandparents also were long since dead.

Linda was a short woman, under five feet tall. When she told me that her grandparents and her mother also were short, a detail she remembered from family photos, I froze.

"It was probably my family you saw," she deduced.

It made too much sense for me not to believe it. Three spirit entities--two females, and one male--all extremely short? The spirit-manufactured television? And the fact that the "dream" had taken place in the room in which my physical body lay asleep?

This was the first major piece of proof that I had obtained in my search for truth. So with one successful out-of-body experience to my credit, I attempted another.

Again I followed the method described in the Monroe book, and with some interesting results. This time I was a little bit more adventurous. After I was out-of-body, I found myself behind my bedroom door. I remembered what I had read about spirits on the astral level being able to fabricate their surroundings simply by thought, so I gave it a try.

I visualized my sister Cathy, as a test, and in she walked with a bathrobe on and a towel wrapped around her head like a turban.

I closed the door, and thought of one of my ex-roommates, and in he walked. This was fun. I no longer was afraid of this out-of-body stuff. But the main thing that I proved to myself was that the spirit dimension was real.

Chapter 3

What We Know

The MacLaine book certainly had sparked my imagination. With the out-of-body experience as some sort of proof, I slowly began testing out some of the other theories that were presented. The accumulative effect that the inherent logic was having upon me allowed me to trust enough to explore further.

This intuitively felt right to me. It is ironic that I intuitively felt this, because on a conscious level I began experimenting with this very thing: intuition.

In the past I would mix what I now understood to be intuition with the intellectual process, and my results were hit and miss. More often than not I would get something that I wasn't really comfortable with and end up regretting it. If I followed the basic rule of thumb with this intuition theory, I should theoretically come out ahead of the game. This appealed to me logically and intuitively. The theory wasn't so complex, but as I was soon to learn, it could be subtle.

What for eons had been referred to as "woman's intuition" actually was available to all of us. By and large women tend to be more in touch with their feelings than men, and going with your gut feeling was at the center of following your intuition. Men had the same faculty, but society forced men to put their feelings aside. It wasn't acceptable for men to be sensitive. But things slowly were changing. Blowing us all to kingdom come wasn't the answer, so maybe brute force was on its way out and intuition was coming in.

The faculty for being receptive lies dormant in most men. So like any other muscle that never has been used or has not been used for a long while, exercise is necessary. But before one approaches any sort of workout, some instruction always is beneficial. For instance, if someone were beginning weight training and had no instruction, he could seriously injure himself. By the same token, were a beginning weight trainee not to progressively add more weight to their workout, there would be no new gains. This same principle applies to intuition.

For instance, one may be experiencing the emotion of fear. There are many times when fear arises, and yet we "know" whatever is causing the fear is something we must face. Turning from the situation based on being in touch with the feeling of fear would not necessarily be following one's intuition. Understanding the feeling underneath the fear and knowing that this was something to be dealt with was the true apparatus of intuition in operation.

Conversely, in a survival situation, when one's house has caught fire and fear propels the person and his family to safety, intuition obviously would have been accessed. So there are subtleties.

Just as the weight trainee learns through experience, risk, and by being honest about how much weight he can handle, we learn to trust and discern our feelings and their frequently attendant subtleties. In both cases our respective "muscles" grow stronger and more confident.

My first test of intuition in action was totally spontaneous and unpremeditated. I had been waiting three weeks for a new project to begin and I was running low on money. I finally asked my business associate for an advance. I found this request entirely reasonable, as I was not the one holding up production. The request was met with "serious consideration" but ultimate denial.

In the past, under similar circumstances, I usually would acquiesce to these less-than-desired conditions. Sometimes I'd make out all right financially--when the project finally got off the ground. But it seemed as though more often than not these half-baked promises reeked of thwarted possibility.

This time, when push came to shove, I trusted my intuition, which shouted "bail!" from deep within me. And I did. I have to admit that after I hung up the phone I was a little scared. I had worked most of the seven past years with this business acquaintance, and now I would have to survive on my own. But facing the real world of business seemed a lot less scary than meeting with entities in an out-of-body experience in the middle of the night in my bedroom!

My work prospects were not very promising, and I did something I normally don't do: I answered an ad from an employment agency. The position was with a computer accessories company. I wasn't sure that I would take the job even if it was offered to me, but I was curious enough to go to the agency to at least check it out. I got my wrists slapped for having left my resume at home. But as I said, I was just checking things out, and in the back of my mind I probably still was resentful for having to pay a fee for a job. Working at a job that was not something I was in love with was bad enough! Now I was expected to pay in another way, too!

Actually the job sounded interesting enough. The money--or rather the *potential* income, as this was a sales job--was tempting. Any more information would come in another interview with the hiring company, should my resume warrant an interview.

So I was back to this little matter of a resume.

"You know that resume that I left at home," I began surreptitiously. "Well," I paused, "there never was one."

"I'm not so surprised," the counselor smiled.

Without flinching, the counselor directed me to a woman in the same building who did resumes. I was asked to return when I had one. *Shades of Dorothy and a certain witch's broomstick*, I thought.

I was in a pretty good mood. I was doing detective work, not job hunting, so I didn't mind dropping in on this resume lady. The resume lady, as I then called her, shared an open suite of offices with an attorney and some other professionals. The hardwood floors and the adobe corner fireplace made the atmosphere warm. But it was the sparkle in Nancy's sand-speckled pale blue eyes and her unpretentious, engaging manner--a departure from the starchy snow queen at the agency I had just left--that let me know that I was in the right place.

Nancy made the business of getting outfitted with a professional resume painless and easy. Beneath her necessary business facade I sensed life, so I began wildly telling her of the MacLaine book and my experiences thus far.

"You're the second person this week to recommend that book to me. Let me make myself a little note so I can pick it up."

Little did we know that this meeting would lead to a lasting friendship.

I bounced back into the agency to pursue the computer job the next day with resume in hand.

A few days passed. I hadn't heard from the agency. This really surprised me, considering I had the required experience for the job. When I finally reestablished contact with the agency, I learned that the computer company had not found, in their minds, any qualified applicants from the agencies offerings and promptly pulled the work order.

I was more baffled than angry when I slowly hung up the receiver, but I was a little relieved, too. This meant there would be no agency fee, and at least I now had a good resume that was sure to land me something. I also had a new friend in Nancy, the resume lady.

Chapter 4

Vestitures: Trick or Treat?

Shortly after my first out-of-body experience, my parents paid me a visit from New York. Since I was deeply involved with researching the MacLaine book and seeking experiences of my own as some sort of proof, the timing of my parents' visit was most inappropriate for me.

Their visit had been planned for months, and at a time when being involved with all this "stuff" (as I then called it) was the furthest thing from my mind. I couldn't call and tell them not to come.

However, I did urge them to read the book prior to their visit. The possibility for us to have some meaningful discussion was something I longed for. I obviously felt that the material in the MacLaine book was important, and possibly life altering. I would want to share these possibilities with two of the people I loved most in the world. But they did not read the book. My mother did begin reading it, but had not yet reached the bulk of the philosophies that I wished to discuss. I wasn't holding it against my folks for not reading the book, it was just that we saw each other so seldom and I felt extremely disappointed at this wasted opportunity.

I couldn't very well explain the entire text to them and expect it to have the same effect that it had on me. I still was researching. I didn't understand all that I had read. So to attempt this would possibly set me up for attack.

I could well relate to the alienation that MacLaine felt from friends and peers as she went further out on her limb. I had already put an end, a temporary end as it turned out, to a close friendship of ten years as a result of my wanting to stay open in my exploration. It was difficult enough for me to trust, muster courage, find resources, and evaluate all that I was to discover. I didn't need additional doubting Thomases leaning over my shoulder. I had myself.

My parents arrived toward the end of October. The days were warm and sunny, the evenings California cool. Since I still was out of work, I had plenty of time to spend with them.

We ate out a lot. We soaked up the sun and afternoon cocktails on the newly refurbished wharf. We walked the lawns of the old courthouse, a Santa Barbara landmark. In short, we had a leisurely time of it. I drifted in and out of each day feeling free of responsibilities. Halloween was approaching.

In recent years I slowly had ducked out of Halloween consciousness. The noisy, crowded bars and parties that I used to frequent no longer appealed to me; I don't know that they ever really did. I guess I didn't want to feel left out or left alone.

Primarily, I found myself unconsciously donning the costumes representative of that which I fantasized myself being on Halloween. I would exaggeratedly dress these past few years as a rock star. My dream was to get my songs published, sign a record deal, deliver my music to the masses, and travel. The frustration I felt from continuing to work at jobs that I basically hated and the depression that I felt from knowing I was not a successful musician caused me to personally boycott Halloween.

This year, my parents' visit, and shopping for a gift for my mother's birthday (which falls on the day after Halloween), further distracted me from observing the obnoxious day.

I had been sleeping in the living room, allowing my parents to occupy my bedroom for the extent of their visit. Halloween night was no different. What was different was what I experienced that evening in the dream state.

When I was a child I had nightmares quite frequently. As an adult the occurrence of these dreams became less and less frequent. In fact, prior to this night I couldn't remember the last time I had experienced one, much less one so intense. It was so intense that upon abruptly waking, I ran from room to room and turned on all of the lights in the house.

In the dream there was a man who looked like Salvador Dali. He was holding an artist's tool with a wooden handle at one end and a long thin nail or deathly sharp needle that protruded about two feet at the other end.

People who seemed to be sleepwalking would impale themselves on this pointed object. The Dali-like man, complete with eccentric waxed mustache, then would slit them up the middle from their guts to their throats while exclaiming "vestitures, vestitures!" in his glee.

After each body fell to the floor, he would slash another victim in a similar manner, again wildly screaming "vestitures! vestitures!" as if he were avenging them. With eyebrows arched high and face pinched, he'd slit another. Then another. "Vestitures, vestitures!" he'd gloat.

I sat up on the couch, lights still on, with my heart racing. This dream was incomparable madness and seemingly so real. I sat there for at least 15 or 20 minutes. When the anxiety dissipated I turned off the lights and resumed my sleep.

The next morning, in the safety of daylight, I attempted to make some sense of the nightmare. I found a few things about it a little suspect. For instance there was no blood in the dream. With all of the implied gore that had so overtly shocked me into waking, there was absolutely no blood or even screams from the victims.

The other thing that I noticed that I found odd was this word "vestitures." I had never heard this word before. How could it have crept into my consciousness, and what did it mean? I went scurrying to my dictionary. It was not a very good one and did not contain the word.

I shared the dream with my folks. They made as little sense of it as I had and dismissed it as "just a nightmare." I had a sense, a feeling that I was learning to trust, that there was more to it than that.

Chapter 5

Creating on the Inner Planes

"Ask and ye shall receive."
--John 16:24

My parents returned to New York and I returned to job hunting. At this time I began reading *Seth Speaks*, a book containing large volumes of channeled information received through medium Jane Roberts by an entity now in spirit named Seth.

Late one evening I finally reached the middle of the dense text. The idea that intrigued me was that in the spirit realm everything is manifested by thought. I remembered this concept also from the Monroe book--with the superimposed television over my guitar amplifier. It appeared that in the spirit dimension whatever one thinks is what one receives. After passing into the spirit world, if you think of an apple you get an apple. If you think of a devil you'll create that reality. Mind is always the builder in the law of manifestation.

Since our spiritual aspects always are present with us, the same principle applies for us. We, too, have the power to manifest whatever it is that we desire. This is why positive thinking works. It is why affirmations work. The only difference between the spirit world and ours in this regard is that due to our being encumbered in the physical, it may take us somewhat longer than those in spirit to manifest that which we desire.

Since I had been lucky enough to have some pretty remarkable experiences thus far, I decided to investigate further by testing out the validity of this challenging new material. So I laid the book down upon my chest and asked for five specific things to come to fruition in the next 24-hour period. I figured that if this concept really was true, I might as well get my proof in spades, so I went for broke in my requests.

First I asked for another interesting experience to occur in the dream state. I had had a few already and was hungry for more. I didn't want to have to rely so much on the rationalization process, so I next requested some sort of physical proof to materialize. I had been having difficulties with one of my roommates, so I asked for that situation to be resolved. Since I was a musician and I always was looking for more direction in that area, I asked for something to happen regarding music. Finally, I asked for something promising to come to me in the way of much-needed employment.

Before bed I decided to watch television. So I put the book down, switched on the set, and sprawled out on the couch. I kept seeing those brightly glowing horizontal lines that one sees after having read for a number of hours. I watched the screen in a daze. I was almost too tired from all of the reading to even get up and go to bed. My mind was racing with the newly read possibilities, but the rest of me was numb.

For some reason a friend who had moved to Florida some years earlier popped into my thought stream. I hadn't seen him since he had left or kept in contact with him in any way. At the time I was too tired to analyze this. I just lay receptive to these floating thoughts.

Then the telephone rang.

I jerked suddenly because of this glaring, intrusive clamor. In my stupor, it took me a second to register that it was the phone that had rung. It felt more like a fire alarm going off in my head. I groggily retreated to my bedroom from where the jolting sound emanated and silenced the beckoning racket.

It was a friend who was relocating the next day to another state calling to remind me of a breakfast date we had set for the next morning. I had totally forgotten about the date. There obviously were other things on my mind.

"What time...eight o'clock...in the morning? What time is it now?" I wanted to know.

"But that's in six hours!" I protested.

"No I can't, I'm beat. How 'bout eleven?"

She wasn't buying it.

"But I don't want to get up that early. It's practically the middle of the night, for God's sake."

She was unrelenting, and I was totally exhausted.

"You're out of your mind.... I know you're moving...of course I want to see you."

I was contemplating saying good-bye right there on the phone, but that would have been tacky. We were good friends and I should see her off, even if it meant not necessarily being in my body for the occasion.

"Okay," I finally said begrudgingly.

"I'll meet you at eight....Where again? Okay...can we talk later? I've got to get to bed. See you then. Bye."

When I woke from my six-hour nap, I threw on some clothes and scooted out the door. Cindy already was seated at an outside table at the near-empty eatery when I arrived. When the waitress came to take our orders I said, "No coffee for me. I'm going back to bed when I get out of here."

"Oh, do you work nights?" she asked empathetically.

"No."

The waitress laughed, shook her head, and left the scene.

I was feeling a little bit more awake. I chatted with Cindy about her move, the route she would take, and all her new plans. And by the time our food had arrived, the restaurant was full.

Two men had just seated themselves at a table to our left. I recognized the young man who was facing me. Being somewhat of a people watcher, as many writers are, I turned my head to survey the other diners out on the patio with us. I almost did a double take when I found myself seated across the narrow aisle from my friend who had moved to Florida--the same friend who had crossed my mind just six hours earlier!

"Hi, Jon, when did you get in?" I found myself asking in shock. I was too tired to give him any information on my latest foray into "the hidden" (the occult), so I failed to mention this recent bit of precognition. I didn't think it would mean anything to him. I didn't yet know what, if anything, it meant to me. But it felt strange.

Cindy and I resumed our conversation. She was anxious to hit the road. So we quickly finished what remained of our meal, hugged each other, and said our good-byes.

"You'd better write!" I said as I tickled her waist.

"Oh, I will...Stop!," she laughed gasping for air.

The house was quiet when I returned home. Since I was more awake by this time, I didn't go back to bed as I thought I would. Instead, I found myself pursuing the want ads.

I spotted a somewhat interesting ad, called the number, and set up an interview for later in the day. It was to take place at three o'clock.

I went to the bathroom to shower and encountered the roommate that I was on the outs with. Quite spontaneously we found ourselves embracing each other and making apologies.

Walking back to my bedroom through the dining room, I stopped in my tracks. I paused, realizing that two of the things I had asked for--the potential job and the roommate rectification--already had taken place. And it wasn't even noon yet! Maybe getting up early was a good thing after all. By concerning myself with the events of the previous evening, I then was made to chillingly relive something I had just gone through in the dream state.

In the dream--if that's even what it was, it seemed so real--I was working on a space station, floating on the outside of it just off the moon. When I looked toward the earth, the sense of my distance from it frightened me. The feeling of being swallowed up--drowning in space--was so great that I had to return immediately. I remember waking with a start sometime in the middle of the night. I physically jumped up in bed in a wavelike motion. What I had imagined that to have been was the shock that one experiences from coming back into one's body too quickly. In fact, it was identical to the feeling I had when returning to my body the night I had journeyed out of it.

With this memory--the third completed manifestation of the five that I had requested--I showered, shaved, and began dressing.

Our bathroom mirror was quite large, with dressing room lights adorning it on all sides. This factor brought into focus minute details that might otherwise be missed. As I dressed I looked into the mirror, and I noticed that my hand was dirty. It looked as though there was some kind of grease on one of my fingers. I found this perplexing because I had just showered. Maybe one of the knobs that regulated the water in the shower was coming off of its metal post and I had accidentally touched the post, which was sure to have had a lubricant on it.

Wherever it had come from, the prospect of having to clean off this mess without contaminating my contact lenses, which I now needed to pop in, was more than irritating. I was feeling especially pressured now because I still had to locate a friend who would be willing to take me to the job interview since my car was in the shop.

Then I stopped for a second. I looked again at my finger, not through the mirror with its trickery but directly. What was so startling was my ring. It was a heavy silver ring with a green malachite stone that I had purchased impulsively six months earlier at a beach craft show. I had worn it every day without ever taking it off. Now as I looked at it, I was shocked to see that the silver had transformed completely to a dull grey!

It was unbelievable. Overnight, the polished shining silver had tarnished. Could my space traveling have caused this molecular change? That is what first came to mind, but I didn't know for sure. What I did know was that this was the physical proof I had asked for.

Of course I was incredibly energized by this manifestation, and I was in quandary as to what it might mean. How could this have happened? What would happen next? I was spinning.

I had some time to kill before the job interview, so I stopped into a jewelry store and then consulted with a pharmacist at another location for possible explanations as to how my ring may have changed color. But based on where I had been prior to this ring phenomenon, none of their explanations were plausible. So at this rather exciting point, I was left to believe that this was indeed the physical proof I had been seeking. I further reasoned that even if there was some logical explanation for this occurrence, it was damned convenient to have happened six or seven hours after I had made my request.

I later learned that there really were no accidents and that Swiss psychiatrist Carl Jung went so far as to formulate a theory in this regard. Jung's theory of synchronicity stated that there always was some underlying connecting principle attached to these so-called co incidences.

Still exhilarated from all that had happened so far that day, I wandered into my then-favorite bookstore. A friend's birthday was coming up. Knowing how much he liked cats, I had decided on a previous visit that I would send him a calendar that I had discovered comprised of interesting black-and-white photos of those feline creatures taken in different city scapes. I didn't have enough cash on hand at the time of my last visit to make the purchase, so I decided since it was on my way to do so now.

There were two tables of calendars on display, totaling over 50 different varieties. To my dismay, however, I was unable to locate the one that I wanted after an exhaustible search. I turned from the tables, about to leave the store, when out of the corner of my eye I spotted a picture of a paw of a cat seemingly trying to claw its way out from under a stack of books. The books had obscured the rest of the picture, which is why I had missed seeing the cat calendars. What I also found interesting was that out of all 50 stacks of calendars, only this one was covered with books.

Immediately I slid the three books aside, grabbed the calendar, and went to pay for it. On my way to the counter, however, a voice inside my head told me to go back to the calendars and find out which books they were. Since I was new to this synchronicity theory, if in fact it was just a theory, I was certainly going to test it out as much as possible, especially in lieu of all that I had experienced so far that topsy-turvy day.

Something definitely was going on. The title of all three books was *You've Been Here Before* by Edith Fiore. I laughed out loud while not even knowing the subject matter of the book. I was laughing because this was my second visit to the calendar tables--I obviously *had* been here before.

Upon reading the back cover of the book, I discovered that this book dealt with reincarnation. It was comprised of many different people's accounts of being hypnotized to relive some of their past lives. The process that facilitated this experience was referred to as "a past-life regression."

I found it so amazing that as I went about my normal day these neat little things kept popping out at me. I was later to learn that "the more we use, the more we are given." I just didn't know how much more I could take! Yet I had wanted to prove that all I had been reading was true.

Of course, I bought the book. It then occurred to me that maybe I was meant to purchase all three copies and give them to friends. So I went back--now my third trip to the calendars--to pick up the two remaining books. But when I got there they had mysteriously disappeared. This was one mystery I never was able to solve. But that was all right. For the moment I had my hands full.

I arrived back home in plenty of time to dress for the interview I had set earlier that morning. I was thankful to have found a friend whose day off was Mondays and who agreed to take me to the interview so that I would not have to deal with the laborious public transportation system the provincial beach town had to offer.

When my friend arrived, I began excitedly telling him of the day's events. He was a fairly open person, yet there was that skeptical side glance he would occasionally throw me that said, "sure, Steve," as I continued my episodic stories en route to the place of my hopeful future employ.

Within minutes we reached our destination. I departed the vehicle rather deliberately, causing my friend to ask if I was all right. I then told him of the oddest sensation I was experiencing in my throat and in the area between my eyebrows. It was a tingling, vibrating sort of feeling. It was as if I had swallowed a fly, still alive, that was furiously flapping its wings to escape this larynx dungeon.

"Maybe you're coming down with the flu," my friend offered, trying to be helpful.

I kept swallowing in hopes of drowning the sensation, only then to be made more aware of the vibrating on my forehead. It was not an unpleasant feeling. In fact, it was pleasurable in a way. The vibrations at least succeeded in temporarily diverting my attention from the anxiety I was feeling as the hour for the dreaded interview drew closer. So I took it as a sign of some kind and entered into a pre-interview pep talk with myself.

Steve, I told myself, *keep your mouth shut, and let your spirit do the talking*.

Since I still was so new to all of this at the time, I hadn't a clue as to what these vibrations were all about. I was later to learn that I was opening up two of my chakras: the throat and third-eye chakras. I had heard the word before but had not previously had any experience with them. These chakras were energy centers in our bodies. The Sanskrit translation from which the word is derived means "wheel." There are seven major chakras in our etheric bodies--the subtle body. However, there are many minor chakras throughout our bodies. All I knew was that things certainly were spinning, all right. Most of this was exciting fun, even if it was a bit perplexing.

Still buzzing, I closed the car door, thanked my friend for the ride, and headed toward the modern smoked glass and stone building. The three o'clock interview was to take place on the third floor of the building, the top floor. Being slightly squeamish about elevators, I opted for the stairwell. The climb up the three flights also would help extinguish some of the nervous energy I was feeling as the interview drew closer.

Moving rather quickly so as not to be late, I reached for the stairwell door. In my haste I accidentally pulled open the glass door next to the stairwell door. The inviting decor of blonde wood furniture with cream-colored cushions and lush green plants caused me to inwardly remark, *Now this is the sort of office I wouldn't mind working in--* if I had to work in an office, which seemed to be my lot in life for the moment. Realizing my mistake, I quickly ducked out of the pleasant surroundings and scurried up the three flights to the correct office.

I was greeted at the door by a tall, lanky man in his mid-30s wearing a casual sports shirt and jeans. This was the man who would be conducting the interview.

The vibrations in my throat and third eye still were pulsating. I imagined that these were indications that the position would soon be mine. It was also a big relief to be in a casual atmosphere, a work environment that I prefer. Just how casual this office would be I was not sure, as there were boxes littered throughout the suite. The Ichabod Crane-like prospective employer apologized for the disarray, attributing it to the ongoing move-in process.

I followed him through a maze of unpacked boxes that led to a makeshift work area constructed out of some temporary partitions. As I settled into a chair in this little cubicle and began feeling somewhat comfortable amid the otherwise chaotic atmosphere, I spotted something that jarred me from this pleasant state.

On the wall behind this eccentric-looking fellow was a poster. It was quite large, probably three feet by two feet. What disturbed me about this poster, one that I never had seen before or since, was that it was a picture of a space station floating in outer space. It was identical to the one from my experience in the dream state the night before!

I stared at the picture, which featured a shot of earth out in the distance--just as in my experience--while trying to concentrate on what exactly this job would entail. Of course my chakras were buzzing throughout all of this.

In spite of what I was feeling and attempting to assimilate, I thought the interview went rather well. I was more than qualified for the position. I felt that I could get along with this man, and the atmosphere was comfortable.

The interview concluded with the information that a decision would be reached by week's end. Feeling more than confident that I had landed the job, I thanked the man for his time, jumped up from my seat, quickly descended the three flights of stairs, and happily waltzed through the double glass doors to the parking lot. I felt so joyful that I thought I would burst. I felt like a character out of a Frank Capra film. Life was magical! My body was not solid. It was just millions of dancing atoms and molecules animating human form.

After dinner that night I resumed reading *Seth Speaks*. Since I was meeting with such good success from testing out some of the concepts, I was eager to read more. I read slowly for a number of hours so that I would grasp all I read.

Finally, I set the book down. It had been an eventful day, and now I was getting tired from all of this reading. I remembered something I had read earlier in the book as I was about to go to bed. It was mentioned that at night the outside air is full of negative ions, and that it would be extremely beneficial for health purposes to go for walks late at night to absorb these negative ions into our systems. I knew next to nothing about physics, but with the good results I already had produced, it was certainly worth investigating.

I had lived in this particular house for over a year, and it never had occurred to me to even walk around the block. The street I lived on usually was bustling with traffic, and the neighborhood wasn't as pretty as some in Santa Barbara. Maybe these were the reasons I used for not previously venturing out into the neighborhood.

It was a pleasant evening. There was a slight chill to the air. Since Santa Barbara is so close to the ocean, it usually was cool and a little damp at night.

The moon must have been full or nearing fullness, as I remember it being quite bright that night. Even the shadows of the trees on the sidewalk were illumined by this light.

After I turned the corner and left this major street, the neighborhood became more residential. The contrast between the shadows and the light on the sidewalk grew more vivid and dramatic, as there were fewer lampposts and more trees. This lasted only for a block or two. To my right I now was approaching a group of storefronts, small shops. It was quite late by now, probably after 11, and all of the businesses were closed for the night.

However, I noticed a light coming from one of the shops and decided to take a peek inside. In the doorway leading to the back room I spied a sparkling red Ludwig drum kit. There were some people milling around, and the door was unlocked, so I went inside.

The man who appeared to be in charge of the space informed me that this was a musician's rehearsal studio. It was interesting to me as a musician living right around the corner, that up until now I had been unaware of its existence.

The rates were reasonable. I always was looking for space to practice with other musicians. So I took the owner's card and proceeded down the street.

Before I reached the corner, I was compelled to look at my watch. All but one of the five things that I had asked for the previous night had come to fruition.

I had had an interesting experience in the dream state with the space station episode. This manifested request was made even more quizzical and alarming by its appearance in poster form on the wall of the office in which I had my requested promising employment interview.

My roommate and I had resolved our differences.

The physical proof--which was for me the clincher--occurred when my silver ring changing its color overnight.

Now with this little walk around the block and the stop at the musician's rehearsal studio, I then realized that the fifth request had just been fulfilled: something to do with music.

It was 11:45 P.M. In 15 minutes the day officially would be over. All that I had asked to become manifest miraculously had.

Chapter 6

An Unexpected Gift

The next day I began reading *You've Been Here Before*. I absolutely was fascinated by these accounts of people who had undergone hypnosis to relive their past lives. This process was used to get to the root causes of fears in this life, physical problems, emotional blocks, troubled relationships, and other matters. In each case startling, documented results were produced.

The book tended to get a bit repetitious, as case studies tend to do. At one point I heard myself say *enough already*! I didn't want to read another case, I wanted to have the experience for myself.

If I had thought about it, I'm sure that I could have come up with a myriad of personal phobias that may have been resolved through this work. But that was not my main concern at this time. I still was not convinced that reincarnation was a fact, as many people seemed to believe. While my out-of-body experience certainly was convincing proof that there genuinely was a spirit reality, I still had no proof that these spirits necessarily "recycled" back into physical form. They simply could be in some weigh station of some sort. I didn't know. But I was going to find out.

The reincarnation question was the larger one for me. So much seemed to depend upon it. Instead of a simple hell or heaven ultimatum awaiting one at the time of transition, with reincarnation the more reasonable and scientific law of "cause and effect" loomed. This allowed one many opportunities--many lives in which to learn and ultimately perfect oneself before returning to the Godhead. Investigating reincarnation was my next step.

I grabbed the phone book and quickly flipped to the hypnotist listings. I called every name. Not only were my efforts fruitless, but I was made to feel odd for even inquiring. The hypnotists I spoke with acted as if they had never heard of a past-life regression.

Maybe I was getting a little carried away. This is how I was feeling when I exhausted all of the local possibilities. I suddenly felt like I was coming back to earth. Unlike my experience of the space station in the dream state, I wasn't so sure I wanted to come back.

The only person who treated me as if I was asking something reasonable was a woman who promised to call back if she found anyone to whom she could refer me. In lieu of my findings thus far, this seemed doubtful.

I continued job hunting, anxiously awaiting Friday, the day a decision would be made concerning my most hopeful job prospect.

I found a few more books dealing with past-life work written by psychiatrist Dr. Helen Wambach. I found these books superior to the one I had just finished. In *Life Before Life*, groups of people were hypnotized to relive the events surrounding their births. The statistics carefully were documented, and surprisingly enough the majority of the cases reported similar experiences.

Those interested in the abortion debate, for instance, might be interested to know that in all cases reported, the spirits did not attach themselves to the fetuses until the babies were going down the birth canals, until the time of the actual deliveries, or until the day arrived when the mothers and babies left the hospital.

This seemed to indicate to me that in the first three months of pregnancy--when it is medically safe to abort an unwanted fetus--that nothing is being killed. At worst, an opportunity for a spirit to incarnate might be lost. But with the birth rate in the world what it is, there would be plenty of opportunities left for reincarnation if such a thing truly did exist.

Dr. Wambach's other book, *Reliving Past Lives*, also had a clinical bent to it, which propelled me further in wanting to obtain my own proof.

On Thursday, as I was mopping up the kitchen floor, the phone rang. I absentmindedly had been thinking of one of my friends. After I said hello, and the other party began talking, I told him that he had just been on my mind. Since I was in the middle of cleaning, I begged off and promised to return the call later in the day.

I went back to my chore only to experience this bit of premonition two more times. Two different friends were to call after I thought of them. I was at the point of attempting to think of who I really would like to receive a call from, when the phone rang for a fourth time.

It took me a minute to remember where I had heard this voice who now was requesting to speak to Steve Travis. However, when I remembered, I was delighted to thank her for the call. For this was the hypnotist I had spoken to earlier in the week, now calling with some names of other hypnotists who did past-life work. She had found two people she suggested I call for more information.

She hardly needed to suggest, for after I ended our conversation, I immediately dialed one of the numbers. I had new-found faith. I wasn't alone in my (perhaps) off-beat pursuit.

When the serene-sounding woman answered, I introduced myself, explained how I had gotten her number, and told her why I was calling. I then excitedly spoke almost nonstop of all the seemingly bizarre events and "coincidences" that I had been prey to lately.

She listened intently. She was as amazed as I was at all that had happened. But unlike others I had shared these stories with, there was a difference. She believed me and she supported me. I finally had found another like-minded person. I still was investigating, and now I was talking with someone who allowed me to stay open and explore further. This was something no other person up until this time had allowed me.

After I wound down a bit, two things occurred to me. One was that I hadn't yet found out any information as to how this past-life work would be facilitated. More importantly, why was I calling in the first place? This service obviously would cost something, and here I was poverty row material, still seeking employment!

The woman explained that the regression could be done at her home or mine, whichever would be more quiet and most comfortable for me. She further explained that after I was induced slowly into a relaxed state she would begin asking me a series of questions as a means of guiding me into the remembrance of some of my past lives. Other specifics would be covered the actual day of the regression, as it was not so involved.

Up to this point we had a very pleasant conversation. Now I had to get to the business part of it and then find a graceful way of bowing out of immediately scheduling the session.

"How much do you charge for a regression?"

"Well, usually," she began, "fifty dollars for a session that lasts for about an hour or so." She paused.

"But you know," she continued, "yesterday I had this feeling that I was supposed to do some service to others."

"I had this feeling very strongly," she said rather deliberately.

"And then you called today." Again she paused.

"So if you're interested in having a session, I won't charge you anything."

"You won't?" I asked, a little dumbfounded.

"No," she affirmed.

It was nice to know that there were other people who were in touch with their intuition and looked beneath the surface of things, as I had found myself doing lately.

"Really?" I asked, still in disbelief.

"Yes," she continued. "You see, the universe has been providing a lot for me lately, and now it's time for me to give a little back. There's a universal law that says, `whatever one gives freely will be returned tenfold.' I've tested it out, and know it works," she explained.

"Well, that's great!" I exclaimed. I still couldn't believe my good luck.

We quickly set Saturday as the day the regression would take place.

The woman gave me directions to her home, which would be a lot quieter than my house with my two rambunctious roommates. I thanked her in advance--I was so thrilled--and then quietly hung up the phone.

Things were starting to make a little more sense to me now. I now knew why I had called the past-life hypnotist in spite of not having disposable cash on hand for her services. Part of me, not my conscious awareness, knew that she would offer me a free session. But I was learning that there was a lot more going on than I previously had suspected in the way of awareness.

I was understanding these coincidences a little better now, too. By not purchasing the cat calendar when I first noticed it, I was led to *You've Been Here Before.* This book led to my recently scheduled past-life regression.

Life was indeed a tapestry, a mosaic, brilliantly colored and pieced together before our very eyes. If we would just see it.

When Friday rolled around, I decided to give the man I had interviewed with earlier in the week a call to find out if I had been hired. When I reached him, he did have some news for me. It seemed that those decisions came out of Los Angeles, and yes, they had hired someone. That someone was not me. He thanked me for my interest, and I abruptly hung up the phone.

I was angry! Here I was, trusting, attempting to be open to these metaphysical possibilities, only to be dumped upon!

Yes, there were some coincidental things happening that I had to admit were a little suspect. But maybe this synchronicity concept was just a theory. Maybe my "electoral college mentality" wasn't serving me in this moment. I did tend to look at the world in all-or-nothing terms. In this case, according to me, either all of this stuff was true or it was a crock.

On the brighter side of things, I did have the past-life regression to look forward to the next day.

Chapter 7

A Day in the Life

I was excited and at the same time more than a little apprehensive on the morning of the day that I hopefully would experience some of my past lives. It was like the thrilling and at the same time scary experience I had nearly every time I returned to Santa Barbara by air.

Hovering above the patchy stratus clouds, I almost would be able to make out land. As we slowly descended I tingled with delight at the prospect of touching down once again on my beloved Shangri-la. Then the sense of dread would pass through me.

It flushed from my solar plexus through to my face. Heat. And the sensation was totally irrational. For like a Shangri-la, approachable only through the veil of a time anomaly, I feared we would go off course and miss our coordinate by a breath, never to find this elusive dreamland again.

I guessed that today I would be going on a trip of sorts as well. The difference was that I was going on a trip back in time.

The woman who would regress me lived on the east side of town, a quick two miles away from where I lived. The brilliant sun danced playfully in the deep blue sky. It was a brisk but invigorating day. I loved sweater weather like this.

Since moving to California some twelve years earlier, I had been transformed into a chronic beach person. But as much as I loved the feeling of the sun baking my body brown, it was this fall weather that I had grown up with on the East Coast that was my favorite.

My family and I would drive to Long Island's north shore in the fall, when the Atlantic was muscular with white-capped waves. I'd walk along the shore and collect tiny colored pieces of broken glass that the eroding forces of nature had made smooth. They looked like sugar-glazed hard candies or puzzle parts.

I now was on my way to explore some other puzzle parts: past lives--if there were such missing pieces logged in the sands of time.

Mary was an attractive blonde who I guessed to be in her mid-30s. She graciously invited me into her modest but cozy home, and led me into a medium-sized room. This was where we would do the work.

The main piece of furniture was a cross between a couch and a bed covered with colorful pillows of every shape and size. I was invited to remove my shoes and climb aboard, which I promptly did.

Mary's presence already had put me at ease, but now I was really comfortable. The faint ticking of a grandfather clock at the far end of the room further soothed me into a state of tranquility. If I didn't fall asleep first, maybe I actually would experience a past life or two.

When I had settled in, Mary reiterated the basic procedure for regression that she would employ. First, she would guide me into a receptive mode. After I was sufficiently relaxed, she would ask me a series of questions. When I was in this relaxed state, she also might make requests of me.

Right before we began Mary asked me if it would be all right to touch me at any given time during the session.

"Sure," I said compliantly, but with a question in my voice. With another new stranger I may not have been so willing, but there was something loving and easy to trust about this woman.

"If anything," she clarified sensing my concern, "I will stroke your arm--like this."

She delicately touched my shoulder, softly brushing down my arm to my wrist. I was a bit curious as to why this would be done but much more anxious to begin the actual work. It seemed like I had waited at least a lifetime for this experience.

I don't remember the actual method she used, but very quickly I reached a relaxed state. It felt dreamy. I didn't feel anything unusual or startling. It was similar to laying down on a couch for a nap on a Sunday afternoon. I guess I was expecting a light show or some other form of special effect.

Mary then began quietly asking her questions.

"What do you see?"

"Well, it's sort of white," I contributed. "It has a kind of cartoonish quality to it."

"Something is coming into focus. Can you tell me what it is?"

I strained to see what it was, but all I could see was this white everywhere.

Mary persisted in her questioning.

"Now Steve, look deeper. You're looking at something."

I was getting a little discouraged. I wanted to see something. And just as I was about to give in to futility, it appeared.

"It's kind of strange. I mean, it almost looks like a cartoon. But it's no big deal or anything."

"What is it? Trust what you're getting," she instructed.

"I see a log cabin. But it's out in the middle of nowhere. And there's all this white stuff around it."

"Do you see any people?"

"Well, yeah," I paused.

"There's this granny type of person poking her head out of one of the windows."

"Do you know who she is?"

"No. She looks like Granny Goose or someone."

Mary and I continued our little game of show and tell or rather see and tell for a while. I don't remember when it happened, but at one point things started looking more real. I guess I had gone deeper.

The log cabin now resembled my uncle's summer house in Connecticut that I went to with my family most summers in my youth. I now could see myself as a young boy. The time period was the mid to late 1800s.

"What is your name?" Mary asked.

"Tracy," I answered.

I don't know if it was my rational mind coming through or what, but I then changed the name to "Spencer." I quickly reasoned to myself that Tracy was a girl's name, and I could see that I was a little boy in this particular life--if that is in fact what I now was observing. "Spencer" probably came from first hearing myself say "Tracy." *Spencer Tracy.*

"Stick with your first impressions. Trust what you get," Mary reminded me.

My father in this life then appeared. He was very masculine--a hard man. He suppressed his feelings and forced me to be this way too. We both wore Western garb. He also was carrying a rifle.

"You are now a few years older. What do you see?" Mary questioned.

I don't remember the immediate impressions I got or exactly what I saw, but I did appear older. Then panic struck.

"I don't want to be here!" I cried.

"What is it?" Mary pleaded.

"Fire!" I gasped.

I squirmed, not wanting to view this scene. As I saw the fire, I physically got hot from the flames.

"I don't feel good!"

"Tell me about the fire," Mary persevered.

"The baby!" I spat out, gasping for air.

"Yes, go on, what about the baby?"

"I shouldn't be doing this!"

"Doing what?"

"Playing with my mind. I don't want to be here!"

I was suffocating emotionally. I got hotter and hotter. I struggled to breathe. I writhed uneasily, attempting to escape.

"It's okay," Mary cooed, as she gently brushed my arm in the same manner as she had done before we began the session.

Surprisingly, I started to feel better. The dread had gone as quickly as it had come. I felt relief.

I took in a long, refreshing breath of air. I still was in trance.

"Are you okay?"

"Yes," I exhaled.

I breathed until I felt more calm. A few minutes later I again heard Mary's soothing, reassuring voice.

"Ready to continue?"

"Yes," I answered feeling more relaxed.

"All right," she paused, "you are now 17. Tell me what you see."

It actually was quite beautiful.

"Well," I began, "you're not going to believe this."

"Yes," she said inquisitively.

"I'm in a canoe with my dad."

"Yes?"

"It looks sort of like *On Golden Pond*, with diamonds sparkling in the water," I paused. "But this is silly," I half laughed.

"What?"

"Well," I began hesitantly, "I look like Bruce Jenner wearing a Davy Crockett outfit, and my dad looks like Jed Clampett!" I protested.

"Go on."

"But this is stupid. I'm just making this up."

I had wanted this experience, and was lucky enough to finally be having it, and now it was just me making it all up. This was dumb. What a joke. Then something astonishing happened.

"Oh! You don't know what I'm seeing!" I was transfixed.

"What is it?," Mary asked.

"I can't believe this!"

I was in awe.

"When you're ready," Mary offered, giving me space.

Up until then everything that I had seen had a dreamlike quality to it. It was like seeing something in the mind's eye. There were flashes of vividness, but mostly the images were fleeting, causing me to think that I was making it up.

What I now was seeing, or rather experiencing, was far more dramatic. It was real. It was happening. I was there!

In an analogous sense, everything that I previously had seen was like watching television. But what I now was experiencing was like someone literally stepping into my living room.

The brightly lit *On Golden Pond* scene had abruptly, almost violently, blacked out to the final reverberating chord of the Beatles' song *A Day in the Life*.

Only now, after years of recounting this incident, can I laugh at the literal irony in the choice of music that scored this scene. At the time I was too enmeshed in the drama that this music helped to create to notice the musical pun.

It was night. Black. The darkness made what little I could see of this road from the Old West look especially wide.

Fog, like that of dry ice, rose from the ground. A black stagecoach pulled into view. It stopped almost on que, with the fog still rising. A door opened. I stepped inside.

"This is incredible!," I exclaimed.

"Now can you tell me what you see?" an ever-present Mary asked.

I was looking into the intensely penetrating dark brown, almost black eyes of a man dressed in regal attire. He wore a shiny black top silk hat, black cape, white shirt, and those inescapable eyes!

"It's Abraham Lincoln!" I finally gasped.

I was inches from his face. Despite what history has written, in addition to being an enormously striking figure this was an extremely handsome-looking man.

"Does he have anything to say to you?" Mary inquired, obviously sensing the significance of this occasion.

I hesitated for a moment.

"Yes," I replied from deep trance.

He didn't speak to me with his physical voice, but rather through visual pictures, through what I later learned was known as telepathy.

"Don't listen to anyone," he instructed.

"Anything else?"

A picture of the path that led to the log cabin that I had seen earlier in the session came into my mind's eye, along with the words "stick to your own path."

"Yes?" Mary coached.

"And--know thyself."

"Does he have anything else that he'd like for you to know?"

"That the kingdom of God lies within."

"Is there any other message?"

The spell was fading and I was coming out of trance.

"No," I concluded.

"Okay," Mary whispered, "when you're ready, but take your time, you can slowly open your eyes."

Like coming out of a cat nap, I stretched my arms to the ceiling, yawned, and slowly blinked my eyes open. I sat up, clasped my left hand over my right wrist and stretched forward.

"How do you feel?," Mary smiled.

"Good," I paused. "I feel pretty good, but a little tired."

"Take your time," Mary graciously offered.

I was in a bit of a daze. Part of the eventful hour had been emotionally draining. Of course, the latter part had been extremely riveting if not thrilling. I guessed that with all I had been through, being tired was to be expected.

"I'm a little confused," I told Mary. "I mean, I don't think, I mean I couldn't....Was I Abraham Lincoln in a previous life?"

"I don't know," Mary paused.

"But it is possible. Someone had to have been," she added.

"But it just seems so far-fetched to me," I said.

"Some people's motives for reliving their pasts," Mary began, "are to find out if in fact they had been someone famous from history. That's perfectly fine if that's where they are in their process. But what I feel is important is the information. Especially if it clarifies concerns they are having in their lives." Mary concluded.

"I guess," I said, still questioning.

"For instance, the information you received from Mr. Lincoln. Did you find this helpful?"

"I guess I just have a lot to think about," I said, attempting to answer the question truthfully.

"I know something happened--something major." I was referring especially to the meeting with Lincoln. "And I didn't make it up. It was too real. The vivid quality of the experience. The emotions. It was just too convincing."

I was in a strange space. I didn't know if I was trying to convince Mary or myself that what I had undergone was real. I didn't have anything to compare it to, and I somehow was expecting answers from Mary.

It was difficult to think clearly in this post-hypnotic state. But finally I spoke.

"Yes, I could relate to what Lincoln said to me," I paused. "I've been searching. It's been kind of a struggle at times, especially dealing with other people who aren't into this stuff--and that's almost everyone I know!" I laughed.

"But these strange things are happening to me. I told you on the phone."

I was perplexed.

"It gets real confusing. So maybe Lincoln was right. I should just stick to my own path and not listen to other people."

I sat with my own words for a moment.

"You know, it's funny. I feel something pushing me on. If it wasn't for that I'd probably just let this stuff go. It's strange."

I didn't know what else to say. I was hoping that Mary would have some inspirational words for me.

"Well, I don't know what else I can tell you," she started, "but you know I have to be some place."

I was suddenly feeling the pressure to leave, but I wanted someone to sort out this mystery with me. Mary already had been overly kind and generous with her time. It would have been unfair of me to further impose on her. Upon hearing her words, I jumped up, maybe a little too quickly, and began putting on my shoes. I felt like I was in the middle of two worlds. My shoes seemed like foreign objects now to be dealt with.

I rose to the beat of the grandfather clock still ticking away in the corner of the room. It was so peaceful and quiet here. I felt like I did as a child when at home, sick from school. The only sounds I'd hear came from the old steam radiators and the intermittent sound of the motor in the refrigerator, humming two rooms away. While growing up these became comforting, reassuring sounds to me.

These same quiet sounds impressed me as I followed Mary to the door. I'd take a few steps. I'd pause. I'd survey the room and then look back to the room where we had spent the last hour. I wanted to say something but could not form the words. Again I would stop, as if trying to remember something on the tip of my tongue.

In retrospect I can see that I was attempting to buy some time. I was puzzled. This regression really had affected me strongly. I sensed that Mary knew something, that she had more information. She seemed so wise. But knowing of her concerns, my urgent needs would have to go on hold.

We reached the door. Mary gently opened it. We hugged. I thanked her for the session, and then drifted out the door. It was as if my feet did not touch the ground. I hesitated. I stopped. I turned to her, again wishing to ask something. But instead I just looked at her, my head slightly shaking from side to side, brow furrowed, and with an inaudible question on my lips. She knew. She looked at me and smiled. Finally I spoke.

"But now what?," I stuttered. "I mean, now where do I go?"

I felt lost, like an orphaned child alone in a noisy and unfeeling world. I had just had an experience of a lifetime, both literally and figuratively. Now I somehow had to sort this out.

In addition to the numerous instances of synchronicity I was experiencing, I had journeyed out of my body, and now had relived part of my past. I needed more direction.

I could tell by her smile that Mary still supported me in spite of the meeting she needed to attend. She now opened the screen door and poked her head out as the granny had done an hour earlier from inside the log cabin.

Slowly backing into her home, she left me with the words "Spiritual Sciences Institute" as her final reply.

Then she closed the door and disappeared. Now I really felt like I was in a mystery. Spiritual Sciences Institute? I never had heard of it. What was it? A church of some kind? a school?

I felt like I was engaging in espionage, and the utterance of these words was some sort of code name of which I was supposed to have had prior knowledge. I did not.

It already was getting dark when I returned home from Mary's house. With the burning rays of the fall sun now spent, it actually was chilly. Perhaps it was just me. I couldn't quite get warm enough. Of course I would have been blind not to have realized that I still was quite shaken up from the afternoon's highly charged activity.

I felt foreign in my own environment. Somehow it was easier for me to be in an unfamiliar place like Mary's house than at home alone and confused, with the unexpected pulsating residual feelings from having endured a past-life regression.

I had been deeply moved. Devastated. Shocked. Touched. Awed. Blessed.

The experience was so genuine that I was convinced that something or someone had gone to a lot of trouble to make their presence known to me. I was supremely baffled and physically exhausted. I felt as if I had stayed up all night. I was wiped out. Was this time-warp lag?

I had no idea these regressions could be so grueling. I had no idea that I would go anywhere or experience much of anything. Now I was left to deal with the aftermath alone.

Was I Lincoln/wasn't I Lincoln? Who cared? My point for undergoing the regression was to prove or disprove reincarnation. If someone had preached reincarnation to me before I read the MacLaine book, I would have thought it meant coming back as an ant and pooh-poohed it. Now, with this powerful experience, I had to start looking at it more closely.

Chapter 8

A Pocketful of Miracles

Come Sunday I was back in my latest hangout--the want ads. There was only one position that seemed a possibility. I circled it and intended to call first thing the next morning. Based on the information in the job description, I was qualified for this particular job although I wasn't too crazy about the work. Ten years of it had burned me out.

On Monday morning I thought I'd be smart. I would call the perspective employer 15 minutes earlier than the requested time to get a jump on things. My financial situation was getting progressively worse, so I needed any edge that I could get.

When I went to make the call, however, I witnessed a curious thing. There was no phone number in the ad, no company name, and no address. Had I been more adept at my psychic abilities at the time, I may have been able to retrieve the needed information from the ethers, but instead I growled under my breath in my frustration.

Job hunting wasn't much fun in the first place. Now there was this little mystery to deal with. Was this any indication of how the rest of the week would shape up? If so, I was thinking that a trip back to the 1800s might be more preferable.

I still was waking up and not too clear-headed at this inauspicious moment. But when my anger subsided, something came to me from out of the blue.

I had placed ads before. I even had sold advertisements for different types of publications. I then remembered that for billing purposes the company name, address, and phone number were required! With this insight I placed a call to the classified department of the newspaper to procure the missing information.

Unfortunately, the woman in the classified department was having trouble following my logic. She seemed to be your basic "Edith Bunker" variety of person. In my growing impatience, I demanded to know how many others had this job function. She told me that there were three of them. I then insisted that she confer with her peers to discover which one of them had taken the job order, and then call me back immediately with this important information.

How inane! I thought to myself, *My possible future in the hands of a moron!* It stung to think that this person was working while I was not.

Without any other prospects to follow up on, I decided to channel my anger more constructively. So I went to the gym to work out. I was angry.

The workout was just what I needed. I worked hard, pretending that it was my job. By the time I reached the "prune stage" while soaking in the jacuzzi, I totally had forgotten about the events earlier that morning.

Maybe that is why I was a little surprised to find a note left by one of my roommates for me when I returned home. It was a message from operator 22 with a phone number. That poor woman who I had so unfairly vented my anger and frustration at actually did as I had asked her to do.

Being in a more receptive frame of mind, I then remembered that 22 was one of the master numbers. In numerology, double-digit numbers always are reduced to single digits except for the numbers 22 and 11. These were the master numbers.

For instance, 14 would be reduced to a 5 simply by adding the 1 and the 4 together. The two 2s in 22 would not be added together to arrive at 4. It simply remains a double-digit number, as does 11.

I didn't know that much about numerology, but I did know that numbers, like everything else, carried a certain vibration. Receiving a message from someone who carried a master number was an auspicious omen. With access now to this much-needed phone number, I collected my thoughts and made the call.

When the prospective employer finally was on the line, I informed him of my experience, how qualified I was for the job, and how interested I was in speaking with him further in a personal interview. I wasn't going to let the opportunity slip by without informing him of the missing phone number from his ad in the newspaper.

The reception I received was more than I could have hoped for. The man was speechlessly flabbergasted as to how I was able to locate them! He was sincerely grateful to have received the call for another reason, too.

It seemed that he had hired a management consultant to assist with the future direction of his company--a computer accessories corporation. The consultant, whose time I imagined to be fairly valuable, had made a special trip of more than 100 miles specifically to assist in the hiring process of this newly created position. I was the lone wolf who had the street smarts to make his visit worthwhile.

When the excitement dissipated a bit, a 3 P.M. interview was arranged. I ecstatically hung up the receiver and yelped a triumphant "yeeeeow!"

In retrospect I found that I had to seriously look at my behavior that morning. I had reacted quite angrily, causing myself, and even the woman at the newspaper, unnecessary stress. I also found that there was some kind of crazy order to the universe if I could simply let go and let it unfold.

Instead of cursing the darkness the previous week when I lost the other job opportunity, or losing my temper when there was no readily available number for the current opportunity, I could have said, "Okay, what's going on here? What's in here for me? Where's this going?"

The lessons of patience and trust were obviously big ones for me. "Gotta have it now and gotta have it all neatly wrapped up or I guess it ain't happening" were the ways in which I was used to perceiving my reality.

With this new insight I realized that life really was a mysterious adventure. As promising as this new opportunity appeared to be, I wasn't going to count on it. Or at least I would try not to count on it. I would take it where it led and find my next step from there.

Later, as I began dressing for the interview, I began thinking about what I would ask for in the way of compensation should the topic come up. Having had a couple of weeks of job hunting under my belt, I felt more confident than usual, even about the interviewing process. I realized that I was in the position to call the shots, especially in this particular case, considering that I had the savvy to find the missing phone number and had all of the qualifications that were required. There was a strong likelihood that I would be the sole applicant.

Luckily, by this time my car had been repaired, so I wouldn't have to rely on a friend for transportation as I did the previous week. There also was something symbolic about driving myself to the interview.

Cars often are a symbol of one's power in the dream state. As I was to learn later, the sleep state (which we enter into at night) and the awake state (that which we consider to be real or the true reality in Western civilization), are one and the same. As such, each seemingly independent reality affects the other. In the same way, the spiritual, invisible, and creative aspect of ourselves is responsible for bringing into manifestation that which we desire. So, too, with the dream and awake states in their effects on each other.

In working symbolically with dreams, one usually has only the symbol and not always a feeling or specific real-life context in which to place it. But in working with the symbol now, in the awake state, I had a context. I truly was feeling powerful at the same time that my car was working. Part of the reason was due to the recent change of events involving the promising employment opportunity.

I also had a sense that all of this exploring into the spiritual aspects of myself while remaining as open as I possibly could was making me stronger and more confident in myself. With this newfound sense of self--yet still feeling somewhat dizzy from the previous week's activities--I left for the interview.

I'm the type of person who doesn't pay much attention to the route, the different streets involved and directions in general when someone else is doing the driving unless, of course, it is specifically requested of me. I just get lost in the scenery, conversation, or music that might be playing.

Since I was driving myself, it took that same strange vibrating in my throat and between my eyebrows to alert me that something strange was going on again. As I drew closer to my destination, the vibrating increased. But I continued to trust.

It wasn't until I actually arrived at the address of interview that I realized why this particular address seemed so familiar. It was the same building that I had been to the previous week at exactly the same time for the other job interview!

I obviously had brought the other address by mistake. That at least made more sense. So now I needed to return home, get the correct directions, and be late for the interview. Terrific.

I then noticed that I had written the address of this building on the same sheet of paper my roommate had left me with the operator 22 information! Puzzling.

I took a deep breath, left my car, and with more than just a faint sense of déja vu, entered this homage to granite and glass once more.

There were only three or four suites on the first floor, so the office was easy enough to find. But what wasn't so easy to find were words to describe the feelings I had as I entered the office with the blonde wood furniture and cream-colored canvas cushions that I had mistakenly entered on my last visit to this building!

This is unreal! I thought to myself. *No one will believe this! I don't believe this! How can this be happening? Maybe I'm dreaming.*

I probably could have accepted this bizarre situation more easily had it been an isolated incident. But this strange tingling on both visits? the space station scene on the wall of the other office? the calendar incident with the past-life book? getting this interview without a phone number in the ad? my ring changing color? all in the course of a week?

Most job interviews last approximately 20 to 25 minutes. At the time I begged off to attend to a previous commitment (actually to pay the phone bill to avoid cutoff), I had been sitting with these two men for nearly two hours. Almost the entire time I had a feeling of déja vu.

I would look at one man. The other would quiz me on something. I would pinch myself every so often to remind myself that I wasn't dreaming, that this actually was serious business although it was hard for me to take seriously.

I just wanted to be able to tell these men of my strange adventures. Whatever they were asking me was totally trivial compared to what I had been going through. What made it all the more trivial-- without meaning to sound too self-assured or pompous-- was that I knew after the first belabored question that I was asked that I could more than handle the position.

But, of course, since I really needed this job, or rather the money I would make at it, I had to play it straight and play the game that they seemed to enjoy playing with me.

Maybe it wasn't a game. Maybe through all I had been experiencing as of late I was appearing a bit spacey. I was certainly feeling a bit spacey. If this was the case, maybe these men were not convinced of my capabilities.

After spending nearly two hours in this interview, I called it to a halt. I wasn't going for power points here. I really did have to pay a bill or have my phone turned off. Since someone from the company I now was interviewing with would be calling the next day with the verdict, it would be an especially inopportune time to be without a phone.

I found this to be another interesting way that the universe worked to support me. What I first had viewed as an inconvenience--

having to wait for the last minute for a roommate to come up with their share of the bill--in split-second timing turned into a plus. My abruptness and urgency in closing this cozy little meeting may have reeked of hubris, but since this was a sales position for which I was applying, it may have nicely capped my interview performance.

This time I was really on a cloud when I again found myself in the parking lot. I looked back at the building, grinned, and shook my head in utter amazement and disbelief. Finally, I threw my hands up, turned on the edge of my boot heel, and merrily pranced back to my dilapidated vehicle.

The next morning I rose early to be prepared for the phone call. I shook off the grogginess, which was easier than usual considering my excitement. I made some coffee and began my vigil.

By 9 A.M. I had finished breakfast. I had the house to myself. My two roommates were out and about, which guaranteed that I would not miss the call since we were a one-phone household with no call waiting.

I was expecting the call by 9 A.M. sharp, but this did not happen. So I busied myself about the house, cleaning up a bit and dressing in some comfortable clothes until it was safe to shower. Hyped up on coffee and the general anticipation, 10 A.M. came. Then 11.

By lunchtime I began having doubts. Maybe I was too aggressive in the interview. Maybe I was too overconfident. Maybe I did appear spacey. Maybe I was duping myself with all of this psychic stuff. I certainly was alienating some friends. Was that some kind of sign that I was indeed "deep-end" material? I didn't know. But I did know something. I again was feeling overly confident about another potential employment opportunity. Again I was lacking in trust--make that TRUST.

It just seemed so impossible to me. According to the books channeled through the typewriter of Ruth Montgomery, this was "schoolhouse earth." All we are supposed to be doing here is learn. Living to me seemed enough! Having to make a living was even worse. Now I was supposed to see the deeper meaning in everything? If this was school, then when was lunch, or better yet, summer vacation?

After lunch I actually took a break from all this and went back to reading *Seth Speaks*. At the time I was hoping for a visitation so that I could give this disembodied entity a piece of my mind if he wasn't already picking it up through telepathy.

Oddly enough, as I drifted back into this ponderous text, one I had taken a break from to read the past-life books, I was given some kind of message. It came in a flash, but it was very noticeable. I was absolutely convinced by the quality of it that it was not coming from my own consciousness. Maybe this was the visitation for which I had hoped.

What came to me was the absolute knowledge that I would receive the call from the computer accessories company at 3 P.M. The previous day's interview, I reasoned, attempting to balance this bit of intuition, took place at 3 P.M. The previous week's interview had taken place at 3 P.M. and on the third floor. So today's call also would come at 3.

The quality of the message was almost urgent, as if it was saying "not to despair." But urgent or not, I wasn't going to let these messages run my life. I already had been let down, and so I decided to be cautious. I would write some cover letters in response to some other perhaps less-promising ads that also had appeared in Sunday's paper. These ads at least had phone numbers or addresses!

I approached my task mechanically. I mass-produced two letters. When I wrote, "Thank you, Sincerely," the phone rang.

Excitedly, I looked at my watch, which read 2:59.

I raced for the phone, grabbed it, said hello, and as the other party began to speak, my watch moved on to 3:00!

The call was from the secretary at the computer accessories company. Why wasn't the president calling me himself, or at least the consultant? I didn't like it. This was the "thanks, but no thanks" call. But that was not the case here. I was being invited back--for a second interview! I wasn't quite sure whether or not it was a finalization interview, partly because the secretary didn't seem so sure.

But what I sensed and trusted was that I had won the job. The "message" regarding the 3 P.M. call was accurate. The sense I was now having, although different in quality from the other message, was of knowingness. This was my intuition, that feeling in my gut. A new friend.

My intuition was accurate. At the second interview I formally was offered the job. I accepted it. It turned out to be the most lucrative position I had held up until that point. Maybe I *would* start letting those "messages" run my life.

What I learned most from reading *Seth Speaks* is that we can manifest whatever we desire. We need first to simply ask, as I did that night when I asked for the five things to happen.

The next step is to state clearly each intention. In asking it is important to be as specific as possible. Had I, for example, asked for employment to result by the end of the week, it is quite possible that that is what would have manifested. I only asked for a promising job opportunity, and that is what I received: a possibility.

I'm convinced that the universe was working overtime to make a believer out of me, and this is why actual employment resulted so quickly. Since I deliberately was testing these theories, I may have abandoned the project out of lost interest had something not happened quickly.

After clearly stating our intentions, we must remain open. We simply do not know how God/the Universe will support us in bringing about that which we desire. Even in my disappointment over losing the first job opportunity, there was something inside me blindly trusting. I think the many inexplicable things that occurred made me able to continue to trust. I discovered that the way the universe works in unfolding our destinies always is perfect. But this is not to say that we simply can sit back and do nothing.

Inside each of us live dual natures: the inner male and female. The female side is the receptive, feeling-oriented, intuitive, nurturing aspects of ourselves. She is characteristic of all of the qualities we stereotypically attribute to woman; the mother spiritual. The male aspect of ourselves likewise contains all of the traits that we associate with men. These include the ability to think logically, aggression, and survival mechanisms.

The way to wholeness and to manifest our desires, since this is what we are concerning ourselves with here, is to be in touch with both of these parts of ourselves. We need to be receptive to our intuition. The more we follow it, the more we are in harmony with our true natures--our God selves.

After we have established a rapport with the inner female and can trust the guidance we receive, we then can allow the male part to carry out the female's wishes. It is in this way that an inner partnership can be developed and balance can be achieved in our lives.

While we may set clear intentions, there still can be obstacles and blocks inside of us--outmoded patterns that do not serve us--preventing manifestation of that which we desire to occur.

We all have these patterns operating inside of us from our pasts. Parents, teachers, and society in general have planted seeds in us, in many cases unknowingly. These "seeds" or early experiences, grow in proportion to us. They are in us and still are very much present in us as grown adults. I call this latter situation "the forest for the weeds syndrome": those negative, usually dysfunctional situations we endured that we can be aware of consciously or unconsciously. In either case we usually are unaware of how these seed experiences and patterns--now huge weeds--color our behavior and strangle and suffocate us from being all that we can be.

There are many ways in which we can become conscious of these patterns and release them. I will speak later in some depth of my own experiences with some of these techniques. For now I will list a few methods available that you may wish to explore and experiment with on your own.

Past-life work can be quite effective in getting to the root of and removing fears of which we are consciously aware. Hypnosis is another way of getting to the root causes of unwanted physical and emotional problems that we unconsciously have created for ourselves. Prayer, talking to God/the Universe, and meditation, listening to God, are valuable tools for getting in touch with and resolving troubled areas of our lives. Dream-state experiences and the symbols that populate the dream landscape can offer a wealth of helpful information in this unraveling process. There are many excellent workshops offered on dream work. However, it is important to work with a teacher who is undogmatic in his or her approach.

There also are many ancient forms of divination available that can give additional clues as to our strengths and weaknesses--hence, our blocks. Astrology, the tarot, numerology, and the I Ching, to name a few methods, are ways of receiving this knowledge. You can research these on your own or schedule a session with a gifted reader.

Information obtained from a spirit speaking through a trance channel medium is another option. When using any of these methods it is important to remember to be receptive to the information that you receive, but to ultimately trust your own intuition as to its validity. By blindly trusting information you receive without going inside yourself to check your intuition, you not only may build up a dependency on these methods, but you also may rob yourself of the opportunities to know yourself, which is part of why we are here.

Rebirthing, a technique that utilizes a specific style of breathing designed to release unwanted patterns stored in cellular memory, can be effective in dealing with the effects of the birth trauma, past lives, the unconscious death urge, what is known as the "parental disapproval syndrome," and other specific negatives.

Traditional psychotherapy also is available for obtaining a more holistic sense of self.

You may wish to investigate "energy work" such as "Touch for Health" and "Reiki," which is a form of hands-on healing for the emotional, physical, mental, and spiritual bodies.

Bodywork, in the form of rolfing, massage (in all of it's variations), and acupuncture also are worth exploring. There also are many transformational "breakthrough" workshops offered that can assist in the process of rediscovering the self.

There is no right way to remove the blocks. It is simply a matter of what works best for you. As the saying goes, "When the student is ready, the teacher will appear."

Chapter 9

Vestitures and Visions

.

It had been quite a thrilling week in the "real" world, but I still was plagued by my regression when the weekend came.

Abraham Lincoln had played a big part in the regression, so I decided to research him at the library. I didn't feel like I had been Lincoln in that life, but I felt that this was the best clue I had in unraveling the mystery. I knew very little about Lincoln; just the basics: he was the sixteenth president, his birthday was February 16, he abolished slavery, he was assassinated at the theatre by an actor named Booth, and we gave this president a holiday. That was the extent of my knowledge on the man.

I had always admired him and could relate very well to his sense of justice because at a very young age I, too, had an extremely strong sense of fair play. But now I was intrigued and had to know more.

At first, when I saw a sketch of the inside of a house Lincoln had lived in, I was very encouraged. It was identical to the inside of the cabin from my regression. But I then realized that most log cabins looked that way, too.

Lincoln's mother's name was Nancy Hanks, which was interesting considering that I recently had met Nancy Hawks, the resume lady. When I informed Nancy of this historical tidbit, she told me that she, too, had been an admirer of Lincoln and always had enjoyed sharing a name similar to his mother's.

I don't remember what triggered my memory of it, whether it was something I had read or something someone had reminded me of, but I then remembered something from the MacLaine book.

Lincoln had been into all of this spiritual stuff, too! He even had a medium named Carpenter who at one point lived in the White House. I didn't know if my prior knowledge of this (albeit buried in my subconscious) could have influenced my regression, but I felt that even if it had--what with this principle of synchronicity in operation--there still had to have been some underlying significance for Lincoln's appearance in my past-life regression. Was it just a voice from another realm sending a picture and a message of hope and encouragement to me, or was there more?

When I was researching information on Abraham Lincoln, it occurred to me also to look up that puzzling word, "vestitures," from my nightmare on Halloween. Interestingly enough, there *was* such a word! It meant, "something that covers the surface like a garment." I then was able to unravel the meaning of the strange dream. This Daliesque man was telling me--rather emphatically--that the physical body was merely the clothing that covers the spirit. Since our real essence is spirit, the body or the clothing--the vestiture that we don in our many lives--is not so important. The shock effect of the dream was only a way of getting my attention. Had it been a more subdued dream, I may not have remembered it.

There also was something else that I was able to piece together as well: a connection between Lincoln and Dali. I remembered something I had seen on a visit to New York years earlier. I had made a special trip to Manhattan from my parents' home on Long Island to see Salvador Dali's latest work on display at the Guggenheim Museum.

The canvas was rather large (probably ten feet wide by 20 feet high). It was an abstract painting divided into a series of equally proportioned vertical rectangles. About 20 feet away from the painting, on the other side of the gallery, was a table set up with many pairs of plastic binoculars. We were instructed to look through the large end of the binoculars, which would create the illusion of greater distance, and view the work from this distorted perspective. Viewed in this way, the immense painting was then transformed into the head of Abraham Lincoln.

I didn't understand their exact relationship to each other or to me, karmic or otherwise, but I found it interesting that Dali was fascinated enough with Lincoln to create this complex work. It was even more interesting that I had received messages from both of these gifted men within weeks of each other, and at a time when I was just beginning to open up spiritually.

With all that had happened, I was extremely grateful to have the job. The people seemed nice enough. I could pretty much create my own space. I had flexibility, something that I practically demanded in a work environment. I again was making money.

The first few weeks were fairly interesting. I was working with a product and market that I never had explored previously, so there was a lot to learn. This helped make the time go by quickly. But at the end of each day I was thoroughly exhausted. I'm sure that abruptly re-entering the work force after a two-month hiatus also was partly to blame.

The other aspect that I know contributed to my drained state was the fact that telemarketing was not the profession of my choice --or my life's calling--no pun intended. Music was my love. I wanted to write songs, sing, and act. I wanted to be involved with the creative process. Telemarketing was done strictly for survival. Granted, this new job paid well and offered some good benefits, but it still would be an interim position for me.

Each night after I returned home from the grind, I would promptly collapse on my bed for a much-needed catnap. On one such evening I had a rather interesting experience. I laid down for my nap in my bedroom, which shared a common wall to the living room. I don't recall what I had been dreaming about or if I had been dreaming at all. But at one point I remember swooping into some sort of temple Superman style.

What made this experience different from other dreams was that it actually was happening! It appeared to be what I know now as a "lucid dream." I clearly was inside some temple that I never had seen before. What amazed me about the event was the minute details that I was able to observe. There were two golden columns at an entrance, and the walls inside the temple were decorated with tiny gold- and green-colored inlaid tiles. This temple had a definite Eastern and possibly Indian appeal to it.

I would have stayed in this fascinating place longer if not for what had called my attention to the fact that this lucid experience was happening in the first place. As the details in the temple slowly came into sharper focus, I heard some conversation taking place. I stopped for a moment and struggled to make out what was being said. At this point I couldn't even make out from where these sounds were emanating. Yet there was something very familiar about the voices.

I then sighed with recognition that these voices belonged to my two roommates. They were in the living room chatting away.

But then where am I? I quickly asked myself in a state of panic.

This split-second change in consciousness snapped me out of the trance. I won't say I woke up because part of me had been awake for the duration of this odd episode. To keep my sanity in check, I got up, grabbed my glasses, and went into the living room to find my roommates engaged in conversation.

"You're not going to believe what just happened!" I exclaimed.

"I was taking a nap and...."

"Steve, you're not reading that *Seth* book again are you?" one of them jokingly interrupted.

"And," I paused, "...never mind."

I decided it wasn't worth it. They just would continue with their joking and diminish what for me was a very real and perplexing occurrence. I tried to attach meaning to this experience, but it was out of my reach.

In retrospect I was angry, as I had been the night I first came close to leaving my body. Now, I had been inside an interesting temple, in an altered state, without the use of drugs and with the possibility of discovering who knows what. And I blew it by waking.

I continued my naps each evening after work, anxious for a return adventure. But nothing occurred, so I gave up hope.

By chance I was in that same state three weeks later. It was like slowly remembering something I always had known but had forgotten. Accompanying this knowing, the scene that I observed became more clear.

I was not in the temple this time, but instead an open hand came into view. It was brightly lit and extended out toward me. As it got closer the image became clearer. There was a business card in the palm of the hand. I got excited. What was this mysterious card?

The writing on the card was just about to come into focus, and in my anticipation I again accidentally snapped out of this trance. When I was fully awake, I tingled with the magic of the experience. But later I was furious with myself for again missing what could have been an extremely valuable clue to the mystery of me.

Was I being too hard on myself? Was something perhaps just goading me on in my search, rewarding me by pulling me closer to the realm of the divine, to God?

Chapter 10

Readings and the Writing on the Wall

I was driving around one day and spotted a sign advertising a psychic fair to be held that weekend. This was exciting news to me as I never had a reading of any sort and was anxious to have one. I told a friend about the fair and we made plans to go on the following Sunday.

When we arrived at the fair on Sunday, we found a little hall divided with rows of folding tables, banners, posters, and readers of every variety. There were astrologers, tarot readers, palmists, and many others who practiced the various forms of divination. You also could book time with a trance channel medium in a room cloistered from the rest of the traffic.

At the front of the room was a table that sparkled with magnificent crystals for sale. It was all so overwhelming for me. I had been without a clue for so long as to where these people hid out, and now I was in a veritable candy store.

I had wanted a trance channeled reading because of MacLaine's interesting experience with them, but this was out of my price range. So I settled for a tarot reading.

The most arresting thing that I immediately noticed about the woman who read for me was her eyes. They were cataract blue. As I stared into her enveloping blue pools, her dilating pupils had a hypnotic effect on me. They changed back and forth from large, black, shining ink spots to tiny grains instantaneously, as if they were lost at sea in her milky blue irises. Back and forth they dilated--like those black-and-white swirling pinwheels used for hypnosis in the 1950s. Entranced, I now was aware that her face (what I could see of it peripherally) was changing. When I first met her I thought her to be in her 60s. But now she shifted from looking 40ish and youthful to 90 and withered through the dance of her bewitching pupils. The aura of mystery that her eyes pervaded drew me in.

I don't know if it was because I still was so new to all of this or because I was so transfixed throughout the reading, but I didn't remember much of what had been said. Nothing impressed me one way or the other.

I was told that I would write a book and that she saw me on the lecture tour circuit. This seemed plausible. I always had written, but I primarily wrote songs. I did have several year's worth of spiral notebooks that I wrote in on whim or to sort things out at times. But this was all I could remember from the reading. Nonetheless, it had been exciting. Just meeting this obviously psychic woman had been treat enough for me.

My friend, on the other hand, was told all sorts of things by the woman who read for him. He was told that he was psychic and very well could be giving readings himself. I found this a little far-fetched knowing my friend. But maybe I was just a bit jealous.

We stopped to look at the stunning crystals on our way out. I naturally gravitated to them. Crystals and rocks always had fascinated me. I was intrigued by a single pointed quartz crystal that had a little rainbow built into it. Impulsively, I bought it.

We now were well into December. I had been working for a few weeks and making money again. I had been reading nonstop as usual and learning quite a bit, but I needed more contact with the metaphysical community.

The day finally arrived when the Spiritual Sciences Institute, the organization that my past-life regressor, Mary, had encouraged me to contact, was to hold a benefit for itself billed as a silent auction.

In surveying the different items up for bid, you would leave your name at the end of a sheet of paper next to the product or described service on which you wished to bid.

There were readings with trance channel mediums (Dr. Verna V. Yater, co-director of the institute, and Kevin Ryerson) up for bid. There was a huge, resplendent quartz crystal; massages; plants the size of trees; jewelry; beautiful, spiritually inspired paintings with unconventionally shaped canvases created by a woman named Beth Amine; and more.

I learned through some of their promotional material that the institute was a nonprofit organization that routinely offered classes in psychic and spiritual development. Dr. Verna V. Yater and Barbara Rollinson, co-directors of the institute, were class facilitators as well as trance channel mediums.

In addition to the auction, there were readers in small makeshift booths in another section of the hall, whose windows revealed a breathtaking ocean view. I just had to have a reading. in such a wonderfully charged environment, so I sat in front of an available tarot card reader once more.

This time the reader was a young man in his mid- to late 30. I shuffled the deck as I had before and handed it over to him to deal the spread. I imagine we remember mainly what we resonate to as being true after having a reading. This is my explanation as to why all I could remember from this reading was that he, too, was convinced that I would write a book. The lecture tour he saw me on, however, was with a blonde woman about five-feet six-inches tall.

At the time of this reading, I had no idea that these prophecies would come to fruition. I was mainly a songwriting vocalist in search of a record deal who acted on occasion. With all of these metaphysical happenings, I wasn't even so sure of that anymore.

All of a sudden I was viewing my life from a strange and different perspective. I realized that even if I were lucky enough to record a moderately successful record, go on tour, and travel, I still would be left with these metaphysical concerns. Who am I? What is my main purpose in this life? How do I find the answers? It's not that I had never thought about these things before. The difference was that I somehow now *knew* that not only was this now urgent for me to find out, but it also *was* possible. Getting a record deal didn't seem as important. Maybe what I previously called my existential quest suddenly had gained momentum and clarity and now was operating in overdrive. Instead of being passive, it now had become an exciting adventure whereby I could get answers through actual experience.

This also was a little scary for me. I reached puberty at age 11, read *Catcher in the Rye*, wrote my first song, and decided to be an actor. I always knew where I was going and found it difficult relating to people in high school and college that still were in search of direction.

Now it was me who was searching, only it wasn't a traumatic thing. It was fun, uplifting, and inspiring; a mystery to be unraveled that could change my very existence. Only I really didn't know what I was doing. I was working at the new job that was my ticket to survival, but now I was on free fall and I was floating.

Chapter 11

Knowing and Loving God and Self

An accountant was hired a few weeks after I began working at the new job. At first, she seemed on the quiet side. I barely remember being introduced to her, if I actually was. She seemed preoccupied. Whether it was with her new position or something in her personal life I didn't know. Her name was Jane.

Unlike the other woman in the office, Gia, an effervescent brunette who could have been a latter-day hipper version of Annette Funicello, it was more difficult to rendezvous with Jane. For one thing, we shared different offices within the suite and had different lunch breaks. Jane still was acclimating to the work, whereas I already had a handle on my work. But I always was looking for allies at a new job, so it was inevitable we would meet.

When we finally did get around to talking during one slow afternoon, for some reason I immediately asked if she had read, *Out on a Limb*. She had, and from that point on we became good friends. She had the same experience as I in being unable to find more information after reading the MacLaine book. When I told her of an approaching institute-sponsored evening with Kevin Ryerson, she jumped at the opportunity and we decided to attend the event together. The class was quite informative and gave us both a lot to think about and discuss.

A few weeks passed. Jane and I went to lunch together. When we returned, she nonchalantly asked me if I was planning on taking Verna Yater's upcoming six-week psychic and spiritual development class. I said no, which really surprised her.

It was easy enough for me to buy books and crystals and have readings without now having someone else as crazy about metaphysics as I was taunting me with still more!

I now had a new partner in crime.

Verna's class was very informal. There were about 20 of us, men and women of all ages. We sat in a circle in a fairly large living room environment. You could sit on couches and chairs, on the floor, or by the huge fireplace.

Verna was an attractive woman of Germanic descent who still retained traces of the language of her land of origin. Her age was deceiving. Since she allowed spirit to channel through her three or four times a day for the readings she gave, she sometimes would half kid about spirit keeping her younger looking. She used this as an incentive for people to develop spiritually, and it usually worked. I knew I was feeling lighter with all that was happening to me spiritually, so there must have been some truth to it.

The other thing one immediately noticed about Verna was that she was not only a bright woman, but she also was totally committed to what she was doing: acting as a catalyst to bring spiritual evolution to the planet. She was accomplishing this through classes like the one in which I now was sitting, through a weekly donation-based healing clinic the institute facilitated, through past-life regressions, and through trance-channeled readings the institute offered.

Verna began opening up spiritually some seven or eight years ago, when she received information through trance channel Rev. George Daisly. The information, along with her emotional intensity, convinced her that she was receiving accurate information that could change her life dramatically.

Verna had been strongly psychic all of her life, and like others she had no name for it, took it for granted, or both. Now she understood.

As a result of her transformation, she left the extremely lucrative but left-brain world of consulting to schools and universities for which her Ph.D. in organization and management had prepared her.

She spent hours in meditation with Barbara Rollinson, who also was opening up as a trance channel. Their vigilance allowed vibrations to be raised; eventually an overshadowing occurred. They could feel the presence of spirit. They got pictures and could feel sensations throughout their bodies--especially in their faces--as spirit matched their vibrations and slipped into their bodies.

Eventually Verna began channeling an East Indian woman named Indira Latari; Barbara channeled an Oriental guide. Later, a native American named Chief White Eagle channeled through Verna, and Barbara began channeling dolphins.

Verna also channeled the angelic realm that when experienced produced a healing effect in many. On occasion Verna would channel the master teacher, Jesus, who brought a tranquil and profound sense of peace when he came.

In 1981 the two visionary women formed a nonprofit organization dedicated to personal and planetary spiritual evolution. The Spiritual Sciences Institute was born.

The class with Verna was crammed with information and experiential exercises. In fact, it was the high point of my week. We began each session sharing our experiences from the week. Verna was careful to give everyone the opportunity to speak so that there were no leftover unresolved questions.

I asked Verna about my past-life regression and Lincoln. Her understanding was that Lincoln appeared since I was doubting the validity of the information I was getting in the regression. She said that in my situation, it was not uncommon for a teacher as spiritually advanced as Lincoln to come through to assist. This seemed to fit.

In the course of the class we did dream work, which I found absolutely fascinating. We did exercises that strengthened our latent psychic abilities. We learned how to observe the human aura --the etheric energy that emits from every living thing--and the significance of the colors it emanated. We performed exercises to get in touch with our spirit guides.

At some point in each class, Verna also channeled information from the spirit realm and in so doing gave us an opportunity to ask questions of spirit.

I remember in one session Indira Latari, the East Indian woman, came through. Someone asked the spirit the topical question, What is my purpose? The answer she received was universal and therefore applied to us all.

"To know and love self, then to know and love God."

When I thought about these words in relation to the way I had been living my life and in relation to the things I was now doing, such as past-life work, voraciously reading spiritual/metaphysical material, and participating in workshops like these, I realized that I no longer was just on a lark to prove or disprove for myself the different metaphysical ideas presented in *Out on a Limb*.

I was learning more about myself. It seemed to me that one needed to "know thyself," as the Greek oracle advised, before one totally could love self.

Through what I absorbed in the books I had been reading, and in the different workshops in which I had participated, I learned that we all were created at the same time as sparks of God, unique individual souls. We existed simply to create as extensions of God.

When the earth plane was created, we were free to explore this new environment, and many of us did. At first we could embody the physical like a costume and discard it at will. But we began staying in the physical realm for longer periods of time. When this happened we found that it no longer was possible to escape the shell of the physical and return to spirit. We had stayed too long at the fair. We had lowered our vibrations for such a long time that we now were stuck in the physical.

There was no fall from grace as the Old Testament would have us believe. We fell from spirit into the physical purely out of curiosity. In the process we forgot who we were--sparks of God.

This made more sense to me than believing in a God full of judgment who would instill guilt--an anti-love emotion--in his creatures. Our mission here on earth was to remember who we were and to balance the karma (not punishment but merely an impersonal scientific law, "cause and effect" in action) that we had in many instances unknowingly accrued in the course of our dissent into matter.

In balancing the karma (or through learning), we then could hope to escape the wheel of karma and rejoin God as a co-creator with our souls perfected. When we as spirit first incarnated in the earth plane, we tried on a costume and were able to discard it. As my vestitures dream reminded me, now that we have lowered our vibrations and become stuck in the physical for a time, we simply don the costume for a longer duration in any given lifetime.

Since we basically are spiritual beings, this shines a new light on death. If we are here to balance karma ("cause and effect") and to remember who we are--God, and living many lives in the process, then each physical death we experience really is simply a transition. Death is a door that we walk in and out of many times, not something to be feared or something to be looked upon as final. What really is transitional is our stay in the earth plane.

But because we are so focused in the physical, a fascination that helped us get caught here in the first place, we tend to be egocentric in our point of view. We still act as though we believe that the planets and the sun revolve around us.

I was starting to have some revelations on my own, too. Those in spirit always were trying to get our attention through trance channeling. I kept thinking about the word "channel." I knew that a trance channel was one who would enter into a deep trance state and allow spirit engineers to adjust vibrations and thus enable those in spirit to speak through them. I then related "channeling" to the different channels on television. And what was television? I started looking at what television really was and where it came from. Did it come from or through the "genius" of the Thomas Edisons? If so, then what was genius or inspiration? When I came full circle in my thinking, I began seriously considering that those in spirit were responsible for this invention.

In an effort to explain their existence to us through the popular practice of mediumship in the late 1800s, those in spirit gave us the television as an analogy so that we might understand how it is possible for spirit to speak through a trance medium, how everything is just vibration, and how everything is connected.

I then thought about movies. What are they but light projected through moving transparencies that give the illusion of a three-dimensional reality upon a screen. Then I thought, *What are we but light beings, little fast-moving particles of matter cast in the physical and giving the illusion of being solid!*

The spirit realm had given us clues as to our true nature with motion pictures, television, and radio. What have we done with them? We've obviously missed what I think were intended messages, and instead ironically exploited the mediums in the process. I'm not saying that there's a lot of junk out in movie theatres, and that television and radio are wastelands, but we have used the media to keep overly focused in the physical.

With Madison Avenue's bombardment in our living rooms through commercials and other forms of advertisement, we have not only missed an important message from the spirit realm but also have blatantly and subliminally been programmed to want, desire, and gorge ourselves with overconsumption by those driven by greed. We now are at the point where we are more divorced from our spiritual natures than ever.

But things hopefully were changing. I was beginning to change.

Chapter 12

Strangers, Precognition, and Time Warp Travel

As I was experimenting more and more with metaphysics through reading and taking classes, my dream state experiences became richer and more varied. I had my out-of-body experiences, the cryptic vestitures dream, and my late afternoon visions.

Lately I would wake in the middle of the night in an alpha state and hear whooshing sounds racing past my ears as if I was flying at high speed. I never made anything more of it than supposing I was again out of my body and traversing the universe.

I used to go to sleep at night to sleep or to escape. Sleep can be wonderful for those purposes, as we all know. But now I found myself looking forward to seeing, flying, learning, and hopefully having some wonderful new experience.

On one night I had a number of experiences different from any which I had previously. They were fragmented, as dreams tend to be, but all of the action took place in my house.

I remember being drawn from my bedroom by a woman's beckoning voice from the dining room, which was adjacent to my bedroom. She was singing the show tune, "Some Enchanted Evening." All I remember hearing were the first few phrases. And I never had even seen *South Pacific*!

The dream felt lucid, as if it were real life, actually happening, as I drifted from my room to the dining room. The voice had a clear bell-like tone to it. There was something familiar about it, but I couldn't place what. Actually it was more than that. I had the strong feeling that I was moving toward destiny, that I had consented to something at some other time and place and it now was time to be fulfilled. Yet I couldn't remember what it was.

When I reached the dining room, there was no one there and the woman had stopped singing. I slid around in a circle to survey the room. I distinctly heard the voice coming from this room and I was determined to find whoever was summoning me. But again I found no one.

As I mentioned, the dream felt lucid, as if it actually were happening. Only I didn't have the awareness that I was dreaming at this time.

I now heard voices coming from the kitchen. At last this little riddle would be solved. But I didn't find the woman who had lured me into this mystery with her hypnotic song. Instead I was staring at my roommate, Teri, and her boyfriend. Teri looked petrified. She was biting down on her lower lip, like a small child guilty of some crime and about to be punished. Her lips were quivering, about to form a word, but it was her boyfriend who spoke.

He told me that Teri had found another place to live and that she was giving me notice. Apparently, for some strange reason she was deathly afraid to tell me herself. I couldn't understand this, especially in lieu of other, more heated encounters we had had with each other. But I accepted what I was told.

Teri by this time was looking more than relieved. She was actually jubilant. Then I again heard the almost plaintive voice call me with its hopeful song from the dining room. I had the feeling that this was something only I was hearing as I dashed from Teri and Bruce, now embracing in the kitchen.

I could feel something in the air but saw nothing. The lighting was different as well. It was as if there was fairy dust sprinkled through the air. Inanimate objects could come to life at a moments notice. There was a full moon brewing through the full-length dining room window.

The door next to this wall of glass magically opened of its own accord, and in so doing its glass panes reflected back the glowing skull of a moon to me as I drifted through the doorway and into the midsummer night. I now was on the secluded, tiny, wood-slatted deck.

The deck appeared to be illuminated, but by more than the moon's wattage. The air was talc, and I tingled when I walked through it. I tingled even without moving. Now the breeze--or something--was playing with me, for something gently pushed me. I fell forward horizontally onto a bed of air just inches from the deck's floor. I could see the silvery moon reflected in the bleached-out boards in front of me. Then it happened. I slowly began floating. I thought whoever was responsible for orchestrating this free-form dance now was returning me to my previous standing posture, but I was traversing the height of the deck.

I could see the wooden platform nestled in the lush junglelike foliage as I soared higher. Now I could see the telephone wires and the roofs of the houses in my neighborhood. It was a pleasant ride. I was light as air and without a care in the world. In fact, I was rising above it.

When I no longer could make out what was below me, it happened.

The force that was effortlessly pulling me into ascension suddenly went into maximum overdrive. For a few seconds I desperately tried to fight the powerful current. But the speed of the force was so great that after it seemingly instantly reached the point at which I could not tolerate it, my body hopelessly flailing, the force had complete control over me. I had no energy even to scream, although there was a frozen scream stuck on my face.

My solar plexus felt like it was about to explode. The speed the force reached in a matter of seconds was so terrifying that it felt like all of the blood had been drained from my body, disemboweling me in the process.

It had been "some enchanted evening" up until this point, but I never did meet the "stranger."

I awoke in sheer panic. After reorienting myself, and with images of the dream/experience superimposing themselves over each other, I fell back asleep.

The next day I vividly recalled my experiences from the previous night. I was confused. I knew that something fairly major had happened. But it all was so jumbled. Why had this voice been calling to me? Who was this? Why had they insisted on playing hide and seek with me? Why had Teri and Bruce been there? What was the point of scaring me out of my wits by abducting me at the speed of light to some other part of the universe?

With all that I previously had experienced, I obviously was open to receiving more. So why couldn't whoever or whatever was behind this energy have made themselves more clear to me?

I went to work that day in a daze. Throughout the day I tried unraveling my night's activities but ended up in a circle. I was feeling frustrated because with my earlier experiences (although they initially were equally baffling) I at least was able at one point to make some sense of them. I further reasoned that since I now was more advanced, resolve should come more easily as well.

Now that I again was making money, I decided to rent a piano as I had done in the past. Although I considered myself mainly a song-writer and vocalist, I did enjoy fooling around on the guitar and the piano.

The piano movers had just left and I was playing the piano in the dining room because I loved the room's acoustics.

My other roommate and her son joined in my excitement at having a piano in the house. We randomly hit the different keys and made up little songs in the process. Then Teri arrived home and joined us.

I had to be careful about who I told about my escapades, and then I sometimes had to edit them. So after Teri and I were alone in the dining room by the piano, I told her a bit about my dream.

I told her of the segment of the dream in which she and Bruce had been featured. Then her usual jocular behavior changed. She blushed for a moment. Then almost solemnly she began telling me of a little cottage she had heard of that was for rent and that she was hoping to move into. She concluded that nothing was definite as yet.

She sounded almost embarrassed, like a child who had been caught telling a fib--not unlike her behavior in the dream.

She added that she was planning on giving notice added.

I sensed that she was feeling guilty for not telling me of her general intentions, which I easily could understand having been in similar situations myself. I wanted to feel secure in already having a new place lined up before giving notice, too. It seemed that there was the possibility for all sorts of friction to develop when roommates gave notice. Any unnecessary stress was unwelcome and only would add to the stress of moving.

None of this phased me in the least, for I was glad to have had part of my dream clarified. As I later was to learn, this had been a precognitive dream, a prophetic dream. Maybe all of the jumbled dream was prophetic and I had not yet met the "stranger." But if meeting with the stranger meant more supersonic space rides, I opted to keep this stranger estranged.

It then occurred to me that maybe part of me had been on space rides before. I remembered those nights when I woke with the wind rushing past my ears. Were they space rides?

Chapter 13

The Wizard of Serenity, Courage, and Wisdom

There are so many possibilities as to what reality is all about. God knows, the organized religions of the world have been fighting over reality for centuries. Even today it is at the core of most of our planet's wars. But living in a technological culture that is overly advanced in relation to spiritual evolution, it is easy to miss the irony in spouting blood and guts all in the name of one's god. I always equated God's definition with love.

Ironically, it is precisely because there is so little true spirituality today that wars rage, and we, the civilian observers, walk unfulfilled, searching, catatonic, through an unfeeling high tech world--a veritable microchip Tower of Babel for all to bow before. All this as I punch my "save" button. Blasphemy.

I had been reading a lot lately regarding reincarnation. The Cranston-Head book gave an incredible historical perspective on the subject. I also was reading the work of Ruth Montgomery, an author who Verna had recommended.

Ms. Montgomery did automatic writing through her typewriter. Sitting at her typewriter while in a light trance, she would allow those in spirit to speak/type through her. The group of entities she channeled included Arthur Ford, who in the earth plane had been a world famous and reliable trance channel that Ms. Montgomery became acquainted with in her completely fascinating work, *My Search for Truth*. Now I was reading more of her renderings.

With these books, my out-of-body and past-life experiences, my astonishing day of manifesting while reading the Seth books, and with what I was learning in Verna's class, I quite spontaneously came up with my own synopsis of it all. It came so fast I was wondering if maybe I, too, was not channeling. At worst I felt completely inspired with what I got.

What I got was disguised as the fantasy adventure *The Wizard of Oz.* Oz was used as a metaphor for earth, or rather "schoolhouse earth," a place of learning, as Ruth Montgomery puts it. Kansas, the black-and-white place in the filmed version of the fable, was metaphor for an in-between place of transition existing in the spirit realm, used perhaps for reviewing past lives, deciding future lives, or simply resting.

The main character, Dorothy, represents "every person" in my scenario. Dorothy begins in Kansas or the in-between spirit realm, and along with her dog, Toto, a symbol of reason, lands in Oz, "schoolhouse earth." She's beginning a new life there.

The first thing she encounters is the Wicked Witch of the West. My representations for the witch are fear (in my mind, a modern devil) and the shadow aspect of ourselves, that is, the part of ourselves that we don't want to admit is there. The shadow is the worst parts of ourselves that we unconsciously project onto others and then subsequently hate in them because we either are unaware or unable to own the projection.

The Wicked Witch of the West is desperately trying to steal from Dorothy what is rightfully Dorothy's: the ruby slippers. The slippers to me represent our free will. How like fear--to want to take from us what rightfully is ours. When fear reaches its peak, what happens?

Glenda, the good witch, shows up. Of course, Glenda is one of Dorothy's spirit guides. She shows up whenever Dorothy is in trouble, but she doesn't run the show. She serves as a guide and allows Dorothy to have her experiences and make her own decisions.

With the help of the Munchkins, who very well could be "the little people" that many people claim to see, Dorothy sets out on her journey down the yellow brick road to find the wizard. What she really has done is embark on a journey to find herself.

The yellow brick road is an obvious symbol for one's path. Dorothy has unconsciously reincarnated, and she now is on her path, as we all are. Who does she meet along the way?

She meets a scarecrow without a brain, a heartless tin man, and a lion lacking courage, all of which actually are different aspects of herself.

She befriends them and encourages them to join her on her journey to the Emerald City to see the wizard, so that they, too, may find what they need.

Along the journey their collective fear keeps popping up. When they finally make it to the Emerald City and encounter the wizard, they find a god similar to the fire-and-brimstone god of the Old Testament instead of the wonderful Wizard of Oz they had hoped to see.

This demigod demands the Wicked Witch of the West's broomstick as barter before any deeds will be granted. In essence the wizard is making them face their fears or integrate their shadows. Yet Dorothy still believes this to be an external journey.

When Dorothy spills water, a purifying symbol, onto the witch, the crowd gasps, which causes Dorothy to operate co-dependently. She feels guilty and immediately apologizes. The shadow aspect of her has such a tight grip that she is made to feel bad over standing up for herself. But when everyone realizes that Dorothy has freed them from their collective fears, they cheer: "Hooray for Dorothy!"

Upon triumphantly returning to the Emerald City with the requested broomstick, the wizard adamantly reneges on his promise to assist the foursome. In essence he is saying, "You're not good enough, you'll never be good enough, and I always will control you," again similar to the judgmental god of the Old Testament. Now the wizard becomes their collective shadow.

It is only when Toto (reason) pulls the curtain aside to reveal the man-made god of a wizard that Dorothy and the others are enabled to come into their power.

Of course the wizard has a diploma for the scarecrow, a timepiece heart for the tin man, and a medal of valor for the lion. These are unnecessary, however, because in the course of their journey they each had gained what they were missing. Dorothy symbolically gained courage through the scarecrow, heart through the tin man, and courage through the lion. Yet she still is fairly unconscious.

She has learned to do service with others but has not learned, even through the promptings of her spirit guide, that the kingdom of God lies within.

Throughout the journey she continually cries, "I want to go home!" Finally, her spirit guide, Glenda, teaches her to meditate to get there. Her mantra is "There's no place like home, there's no place like home...."

By going within Dorothy comes full circle and returns to Kansas, the in-between spirit state. She has completed a life, learned lessons, and now is back with others who look familiar to her from her journey. Thus the reincarnational message that we've all known one another in different bodies and in different lives becomes apparent.

Finally, I would like to relate a popular prayer to the fairy tale.

> Lord grant me the serenity [which was the heart that the tin man sought] to accept the things I cannot change, the courage [which is what the lion wanted] to change the things that I can, and the wisdom [which the scarecrow desired] to know the difference.

The prayer is a request to be in touch with one's inner female (the heart), one's inner male (courage), and one's Higher Self (wisdom).

Chapter 14

Close Encounters of the Spirit Kind

A warm and sunny Easter had arrived. But lately I was feeling achy in my body. On one evening, when my back was especially uncomfortable, I went to bed early. I lay in my bed, unable to fall asleep. As I tossed I realized that my bed felt lumpy and that it actually was quite uncomfortable. I had inherited this bed from a friend, not knowing its history. The bed had been an improvement on what I previously had been sleeping on, and I never questioned upgrading. It also had not occurred to me that I used the bed roughly one third of my life, and that maybe it had been the cause of my body pain. Weighing the possibility of purchasing a new bed, I drifted into sleep.

As I began opening myself up more and more over the past eight months, I began remembering my dreams on a more-or-less regular basis. On this night the dreams were so vivid that I actually was experiencing lucid dreaming. The dream actually appeared to be happening, and I knew I was dreaming.

In this dream I was walking through the house of a friend. She wasn't home at the time. I drifted in slow motion down a hallway that led to other rooms. Light streamed into the hallway through the luminous, transparent white curtains that lined the wall on one side. I had the distinct feeling that the house had been deserted. This was made even more apparent by the bizarre graffiti that I next encountered. Whole phrases were sloppily spattered on the windows in white paint.

At first I simply surveyed the scene as I floated through each room. But as this experience became more lucid, I could not only make out the phrases, but I also felt a deep, solar plexus kind of knowing that these messages were intended for me!

The message that I most remembered upon waking said something like "If you always use credit, you'll always be in debt." It was quite shocking for me to experience seeing these signs, especially, considering that I was lucid at this point in the "dream."

I then wandered into a wild party that was taking place in one of these rooms. The music was deafening. The room was thick with smoke. Everyone was blatantly consuming alcohol and dancing with demonic abandon. There were men and women and these nude, fairy -like nymphs dancing in waves to the grinding "music."

I was extremely overwhelmed and tried to retreat from the negative energy. Repulsed, I angrily cut free and bolted down the hallway. It happened so fast that the nearest vacant room seemed to quickly inhale me onto its sole bed and slam the door shut behind me, enveloping me in darkness.

I was going in and out of a lucid state from the time I entered the party. It felt more dreamlike to me and less like it actually was happening. But now as I covered myself, finally alone and away from the racket, the dream became lucid again--and frighteningly so!

I can remember this so well because after I covered myself, taking refuge in this cozy bed, the blanket lifted part of itself slowly into the air by its own accord and exposed my tight, fetal position body to the night! The blanket rose and fell on me as if I were a tribal fire whose employ was to send smoke signals. Only I wasn't feeling especially warm just now. In fact, I was practically chilled numb!

I told myself *Don't move and they'll go away*! as I did years ago when camping in Yosemite National Park in California. One starlit night I woke in my sleeping bag to witness a huge bear with its hand just inches from one of my friend's heads. I closed my eyes and desperately told myself that this was a dream until I actually was asleep and dreaming.

Only now I wasn't in Yosemite, and I didn't know where I was. Was I in a dream? in my room? I had had nightmares before, but this experience didn't have the same quality as a scary dream. For one thing I didn't feel as though something or someone maliciously was out to get me. Also, this actually was happening. I felt wide awake.

But if it was possible for me to be more awake, then the eerie voice that then spoke, or rather reverberated through my head, would have done the trick!

"Are you comfortable in your bed?" this mellifluous voice inquired.

"No!" I screamed without sound, imitating an Edvard Munch painting.

I felt like a trapped animal. I knew no other way to respond to this unseen entity. I was shocked to my core. Not only could I feel, but I also could see the shockwaves I was experiencing as bands of pulsating light surrounding my body. I intermittently had the perspective of seeing myself in shock on the bed from the door's point of view.

Then there was a lapse of time. I imagine that the intensity of this event more than likely catapulted me to some other state. This did not seem to last for long, however, for I again was hearing the voice. This time it was different.

Due to the shock I had experienced upon the voice's first utterance, and its echoing ubiquity, I was unable to clearly describe or identify it. Now I not only was able to describe it, but I also was hearing it as if it were a broadcast emanating from a radio literally buried within the back right side of my cranium!

The broadcast came complete with the static that accompanies difficult-to-receive stations. Like stations requiring stronger transmitters for good reception, I could only pick up part of the "program."

The broadcast featured a very calming and reassuring woman's voice. But I could not place it. I only heard phrases here and there, because not only was this broadcast fading in and out, but I was fading in and out as well!

I don't know whether it was the overall shock of this experience or what it is that caused it, but there were times when I could perfectly decipher what was being said and others times where it felt and sounded like there was water in my ears drowning out the message. Maybe I was not psychologically prepared to hear the message.

What I remember most from the transmission was that I was supposed to do something. The main part of the message was that I was not to feel special because of this. Special? I was too busy being paralyzed to feel anything! Or perhaps I was not to feel special and privileged to have had this very experience?

Again I heard the barely audible and submerged-sounding voice as I faded back into the broadcast from a probable deeper state. I was feeling wide awake and much more relaxed when I very plainly heard the voice, who I later imagined to have been a female spirit guide, say, "All right, Charlie, now it's your turn."

I was feeling more comfortable about the transmission, so I was quite eager to hear what this Charlie (no doubt a male spirit guide) had to tell me. Maybe now I'd be able to stick around for the whole message.

But this did not occur. Instead, I felt the energy that had been present for the transmission above my head slowly rising to the ceiling, until whoever had been with me was gone.

Since I already was awake and finally alone, I needed to re-establish contact with myself and sort out what had just happened. I still was buzzing from the fading transmissions vibrations and had the sheet and my fists tightly wrapped under my chin.

My eyes quickly blinked open like two wet windows freshly squeegeed and reflecting back the morning sun. I was in this wide-eyed trance when I became aware of the electrical current running up and down my spine. The current was rhythmic and not unpleasurable. I bathed in the almost audible hum created by these pleasant vibrations.

The circuit went from head to toe and ran around and around. I lay frozen, like a still embryo, awestruck. I ran the phrases I could remember in my mind over and over in a loop. I was transfixed by these two concurrent sets of circuits.

I then chillingly realized that there was no spirit guide named Charlie waiting in the wings (no pun intended) as I previously had thought, and that it was *I* who she was referring to when she said, "All right, Charlie, now it's your turn." I was Charlie! But what was it my turn to do? I couldn't hear, at least not consciously, that part of the transmission.

Not wanting to lose even the few details I could remember, I broke free from the mesmerizing spell and began feverishly jotting down my impressions of this powerful experience. Of course, I included the lucid dream that preceded the spirit communication.

Since I had been reading a lot about reincarnation and had startlingly experienced some riveting past lives that for me made reincarnation fact, the lucid dream aspect of my adventurous night was fairly easy for me to unravel.

In my estimation the message in the white paint had to do with karma. "Karma," according to *Webster's Dictionary*, is "the total effect of one's conduct, believed in Buddhism and Hinduism to determine one's destiny in a future life." The message, with those few well-chosen words, was alerting me of the consequences of my possible future actions.

Karma is a cause-and-effect belief, and often the term "karmic debt" is used to describe the actual consequences one must endure as payback for one's deeds. So the message "If you always use credit, you'll always be in debt" was gently telling me that either I was somehow accruing more karma by my current actions (thus the term "credit") or that there was something that I could do to erase what already had been done.

It was fitting, too, that I next would be shown a mad party scene in which the partiers were oblivious to their responsibilities or altogether unaware that they had any in the first place. In a way it was as though I was being shown my options. The scene had a distinct Dickensesque *A Christmas Carol* quality to it.

I opted for more clarity by fleeing the party so that I could be alone and sort things out. It was then that the vibrations were adjusted to make direct spirit communication possible. It was unfortunate that I couldn't get a playback of the transmission in its entirety. But the benefit I received from the experience was the proof I had been seeking about the existence of spirit guides. I now knew that not only was the spirit reality real (in case my outing with my landlady's family hadn't convinced me), but I also now knew by firsthand experience that it indeed was possible for the spirit realm to communicate directly with us.

Maybe I had at last met my "stranger."

Easter Sunday was an especially beautiful day. I no longer celebrated Easter as a Catholic, but I still felt in the holiday spirit. The topicality of the Easter story, with its theme of ascension, was not lost on me with a spirit visiting me just hours previously and then going through my ceiling to God knew where.

The sky was bright blue and greeted with swaying palm trees spangled by the hot sun. Since it was such a nice day, one of my new roommates, her five-year-old son, and I went for a walk downtown. We walked past a small, fairy-talelike toy store. But most stores were closed as it was a holiday for many. My favorite bookstore was open, however, so in we went.

When we were through looking at books, we took the side exit that spilled out onto a side street. It was actually the first street I had ever lived on in Santa Barbara.

I stopped our little traveling party when I spotted a little metaphysical bookstore that I had heard about on numerous occasions but never could quite find. As luck would have it, it was open, so the three of us merrily scooted across the street and into this mysterious little occult shop.

Spicy incense accosted and then raced up my nostrils. I was immediately transported to India, or was it Tibet? I was focusing on the titles of the first shelf of books that I came to when from out of nowhere--like an exploding box of white powder--shot a pure white dove, aggressively flapping its plumage in my face.

Stunned from this sudden intrusion, I gasped for a second as the bird gracefully regained composure and promptly perched itself onto my left shoulder.

I felt honored and in a way blessed by the arrival of this creature, which was a symbol of so much hope. And I was tingling. Yet this Easter theme was getting to be a bit much.

I walked to another shelf, which featured some esoteric Alice Bailey volumes, and without notice the creature on my shoulder darted across the room to its perch, which I now was seeing for the first time. I guess the bird didn't care for Alice Bailey.

The bird left me a gift in the way of a small dropping upon my shoulder. Now I knew I had been blessed! We all had a good laugh, and as comically as this sounds, I really did feel blessed. In fact I was vibrating; tingling. I was light. Everything had a soft white glow to it, like in those exaggerated dream sequences in black-and-white movies where the heroine usually is seen running through the woods in a translucent white flowing robe.

I wiped the dropping aside and went to look at the sparkling crystals that were housed inside a glass case. I was drunk from the incense, and since the dove's mad flight, concentrating on anything required a real effort. So with the last breath of perfumed air exhaled, my little group and I floated out through the doorway and headed up the street.

Chapter 15

Other Lives, Other Proof

The institute was offering another class with Verna Yater and I took it. In one session I remember, we were to do a group past-life regression, whereby each participant would have their separate experiences.

Based on my private past-life session, I found it hard to believe that with a group this size--there were approximately twenty people--that there would be the individual attention I felt would be necessary to facilitate having this experience.

I went along with the exercise regardless of my perceptions. Very shortly after Verna began the guided imagery, I began seeing cartoon characters in my mind's eye, as I had in my first regression with Mary. Then very abruptly the image transformed itself, as it had with the Lincoln episode, and I now was quite lucidly staring close range at a German officer in uniform. I knew this because I was shocked to see a black cross among the soldiers medals. I also was in shock because I actually was there! I breathed in the experience. Nazi Germany was not exactly my favorite period in history.

I also was feeling extreme heat; panic to flee. I wanted out of this regression! It was very interesting but I had had enough. Yet it continued.

Next I viewed a ballroom scene filled with German soldiers in their dress uniforms and a blonde woman wearing a seductively low-cut evening gown who was holding court.

Some kind of panic was about to break loose and I didn't want to stick around for it.

With another part of my consciousness, I envisioned myself exiting the circle of fellow class members and taking refuge in the bathroom as a way of halting the regression. For some reason I thought I would be safe there. But when I opened my eyes I found a roomful of closed eyes staring back at me through their hollows. I couldn't break from the circle. I would somehow break the chain of energy we had created. But I was breaking!

In desperation I then remembered what Mary had done in our session to calm me down when panic had struck so abruptly. So I slowly and lovingly brushed by left arm from my shoulder down to my hand with my right hand, and this mellowed me out.

When the rest of the group had come out of trance, we shared our experiences. What I learned from this exercise was that in addition to not being too crazy about Nazi Germany, that this past-life recall was real. As with my first regression, there was too much strong feeling and lucidity for me to have made this all up. If past lives were real, then reincarnation was real.

This gave me a lot to think about. It wasn't a clear-cut hell or heaven ultimatum as I had been taught through Catholicism. There were many lives. Maybe karma, the cause and effect belief that went with reincarnation theory, also was fact. Even science would be hard-pressed not to endorse cause and effect. I now was balancing my experiential past-life regressions and altered states, i.e. my out-of-body episodes (definite right-brain activities), with the left-brain world of science. Maybe East and West would meet after all.

On another evening in Verna's class, we were to do some psy-chometry work. Psychometry was the art of being able to pick up impressions, pictures, and feelings from a metallic object that another person had held on their body for a long period of time.

The reason for this experiment was to prove that not only are we all psychic to some extent but also that ultimately everything is vibration.

Our physical bodies appear solid, yet should it be possible to stick a human under an electron microscope we would see that it is just made up of thousands of molecules and atoms and lots of empty space. This, of course, also is true of any inanimate object. As such, the person or object simply is vibrating at such a high speed as to give the illusion of being solid.

In an analogy that I particularly like depicting this aspect of the realm of spirit, the propeller of an airplane is used. The propeller represents spirit. When the propeller is not moving, it appears solid. But when it is spinning, it gives the illusion of being invisible.

Spirit also is moving at such a high speed that we cannot always see it, yet it always is there. Another analogy would be electricity, and science is still trying to prove that one.

I have read in numerous places that the empty space between the atoms and molecules of any animate or inanimate object is the glue that holds it all together. It has been suggested that this empty space is the universe, love, and God.

It may be that the genetic code of the soul--all information pertaining to past lives and the soul's direction--is held in this so-called "empty" space.

In objects there also is this empty space. When an individual's energy merges with a metallic object for a reasonable amount of time, their energy is stored in the object, thus making it possible for another individual to pick up information from it while in a light trance state.

There was a fairly large group that night--probably more than twenty of us. We sat in circle as usual. We shared our experiences from over the past week. Then psychometry was explained to us.

We were instructed to pick a metallic object from on our person to contribute to a tray that would be passed around. It could be a coin, a ring, other jewelry, a watch, or anything as long as it was metallic.

When we had decided on our objects, we closed our eyes as an assistant silently collected the goods. She then redistributed the metallic objects and made sure that nothing ended up with its original owner.

Verna then said a prayer of protection and began a relaxation meditation. Next we were instructed to remain receptive to images, feelings, and impressions from the object we were holding and to not rationalize what we received.

After we had ample time to "pick up," we went around the circle and reported our findings.

I had a watch. The first thing I saw was a cloud, like out of a cartoon, in the right corner of my mind's eye. In the cloud was Rudy, a rather jovial man in my class. I was picking up that the watch had been a gift of some kind. I guessed about the occasion as I had not received this information.

To my utter surprise I was correct! Here I had been going to all these readers for this kind of information, and now maybe I, too, had this gift. Or maybe we all have it.

It was quite interesting to listen to the impressions my classmates got from the objects they had held and then to hear the confirmations they received back from the object's owners. It was uncanny! How could so many people show up at this class and just happen to possess psychic abilities? It made more sense to believe that it was in all of us, albeit latent in many.

Chapter 16

Food for Thought

When it came to spiritual practices, diet played a large part for many. Some believed that the lighter one ate, the lighter they would become spiritually. They also believed this was a prerequisite for ascension, which was what a lot of people were pushing for. Through ascension they would transcend the wheel of karma within this life and in so doing not have to return to physical existence.

Many were hoping to get a glimpse of what it was they had come here for--some even had come from other solar systems. Many were drastically changing their diets to accelerate their growth, and many became vegetarians because of the moral implications.

While this concern over diet was not true of every spiritually/metaphysically minded person I came across, I did know many people who had what at the time I thought were strange eating habits.

No meat, no alcohol, no eggs was one habit I considered strange. Some would eat only fruit; others only bee pollen. There were the microbiotics and the macrobiotics, those that boycotted dairy products, and those that had to color balance each meal to be sure to get equal yin (female) and yang (male) energies from their meals.

Since I was exploring my spiritual path, I took a look at my diet. I ate both red and white meat (poultry and fish). I drank coffee with sugar. I consumed alcohol.

I did notice, however, that when I'd come back to work from lunch after eating a burger, my energy level was shot and that I needed a few cups of coffee to get me through the rest of the day. Sometimes even that wouldn't work. I didn't have an alternative for this drudgery.

In the course of my experimentation I decided to clean up my diet a little and see if I noticed any physical or spiritual changes.

Coffee, sugar, red meat, and hard booze were the first to go. I had quit cigarettes after an auto accident some years earlier had left me with only swimming as a form of exercise.

I couldn't swim if I continued to smoke because I would not have the wind to do any serious swimming. Then miraculously, I simply forgot about cigarettes and never returned to smoking. In a way I quit by accident. But I now knew that there really were no accidents.

It was rough at first going cold turkey on all these foods at once. The morning was the worst. I wasn't thrilled with working eight hours a day at a job that was not my life's calling, and now I had to get motivated without coffee!

I tried herbal teas to at least simulate the traditional hot morning drink, but they actually made me sleepy. I don't know how I did it, it was probably just the passing of time like anything else, but I finally reached a point where I was "out of the woods" and could function without caffeine. I noticed that I felt more relaxed without it.

The easiest things for me to do without were red meat and hard alcohol. There always was chicken and turkey and fish left in the meat department, and if I really wanted booze there still was beer and wine. But surprisingly I found that I didn't miss these beverages either.

My choice in friends was changing, too. I became friendly with many of those who also abstained from these things. It was relatively easy for me to modify my eating and drinking habits with the positive reinforcement of my new friends.

I felt lighter. One roommate who was not even into this spiritual stuff went so far as to comment one day that I actually was glowing.

Part II

The Dark and the Light

"I change the world by changing myself."
--A Course in Miracles

Chapter 17

"Be Still and Know That I Am God"

We celebrated our last class at the home of Carol, one of the members of my class. She and her husband, David, were recent transplants from South Africa. Their beautiful home, flanked along the bluffs of the Pacific, was filled with primitive art from every culture. The pieces somehow all fit together and made the environment warm, open, and mysterious.

Carol had laid out a nice spread of vegetarian salads, breads, fruits, cheeses, and nonalcoholic beverages. There were about ten or twelve of us mingling and eating. Most of us had been in the class together. The conversations were by and large metaphysical, as many of us still were fairly new to this "stuff" (as I then called it) and eager to learn more.

Things wound down a bit as the last of the food was consumed. There were seven of us left at this point. Since we were now a fairly small group, we all shared in the same conversation. We discussed reincarnation, spirit guides, karma--everybody had their favorite topic. Then we began talking about meditation.

I remembered one of my first experiences in an institute-sponsored event. At one point we were all called on to meditate in a circle. Most people had their hands positioned palms up on their laps. I mimicked what I saw others doing, but had no idea what I was doing as I had had no formal or informal meditation training.

Now, as we spoke about meditation at this gathering, I was surprised to learn that I was not the only one who was without a clue in this regard. In fact, most of us were in this category. We were bewildered about it all, and yet knew full well that this was a very important part of metaphysical/spiritual practice and soul growth. We just hadn't gotten to it yet.

We spontaneously turned to one another with opened mouths, frustrated and speechless, when Santi finally spoke up. Santi was a member of the institute's healing team and a frequent guest and participant in our just-ending class.

"May I?" he humbly asked, with opened palms.

We silently followed him into an adjacent room that had adequate seating for all of us, and gracefully fell into our places. Santi began with a prayer of thanks and protection, and then asked us to sit up straight in our chairs and to uncross our legs. Apparently leg crossing could interfere with the energies. He next instructed us to comfortably turn our palms up or down on our laps. Then he began a guided meditation.

"Now close your eyes," he gently whispered.

I was quite relaxed. The camaraderie we shared in class carried through to the party. The food was good; conversation lively. Now we were being rocked to sleep together in meditation. That's what it felt like anyway; it was very soothing.

"Now before you, picture a book. This is your special book," he began.

"On the cover of this golden book are dazzling jewels. Glittering emeralds, rubies, and diamonds. Now take a moment to design your special book. You can use your favorite gems or crystals or whatever you wish. But really see it."

He then paused for a few moments. With the descriptions given I couldn't get the gems off my book! It was a stunning sight, as I saw it through my mind's eye.

"Now what I would like for you to do when you're ready," he said, the soft, modulated words falling from his mouth like feathers,

is to slowly open your book to the first page. I'd like for you to see an inkwell holding an exquisite quill pen. Color the ink any color you wish. See your hand take the pen from its well. Dip the pen once and you will have all the ink you will need. Now take your hand to the top left page and write your name--the way you refer to yourself.

"When you have that completed, go to the top of the right page and write the words `deep trance'." Again he paused.

"Now, go back and forth, writing your name on one page and `deep trance' on the other."

His voice started fading. I continued my rhythmic ritual. But I wasn't comfortable writing with this scratchy pen. The aesthetics were all wrong for me to be able to get into this exercise. So I tried a number of creative experiments. I wrote in my mind's eye, on slippery wax paper, only I couldn't see what I was writing. Then I sloshed around in some finger paints. Finally I settled on a bic round stick pen in medium blue. It glided, and that's what I needed to do-- to flow.

I don't remember the transition, but I had stepped beyond my mind's eye perspective and now was quite lucidly looking into a placid pond with gentle ripples. I gazed into the ripples to see what was being reflected. The teasing waves then stilled themselves and turned to glasslike ice, revealing a beautiful golden pagoda. I clearly could see the floating reflection of the temple. But I wanted to see the actual pagoda. So I lifted my eyes to catch a peak, and then it occurred to me.

Where was I? This actually was happening. But where did I go? And where was my book!

I was supposed to be doing the meditation exercise but instead fell into this tranquil scene. Then I realized my folly. I had achieved a desired state with this simple exercise and could not recapture it again. I could not get back to the temple. I was trying too hard.

I now heard Santi's soothing voice come in again.

"Now slowly and gently bring yourself back to your book," he began.

"Carefully place your pen back in its well, and then close the book. Put it back on its shelf or wherever you'd like to keep it. Know that whenever you'd like to, you may return to it."

We slowly gravitated back to our surroundings, none of us wanting to move. After a fashion we began shuffling through the room, giving one another hugs, and bidding our farewells. It had been an eventful evening. My initiation into meditation had me wanting more.

Chapter 18

Dr. Chang: "Phone Home!"

As I got more involved with my spiritual pursuits, I naturally gravitated to like-minded people. Like attracts like, universal law tells us. Consequently, I drifted apart from some of my old friends. It was not that I no longer liked them, it was just that I was finding we had less and less in common. We were vibrating at different levels, and like magnets losing their charge, we were no longer so attracted to each other. I also felt more stimulated and empowered spending time with those who were equally excited about their evolutions, as I was.

One of my new friends was Santi. He was the man who had led the bejeweled book meditation, the night we celebrated our last class, at my friend Carol's house. Since taking an intense communications workshop together, in Los Angeles, we had become fast and loyal friends.

Santi had been studying with the same trance channel medium that Verna had--Rev. George Daisly. With the beautiful experience I had in meditation under his guidance, I asked Santi if he could show me more. He graciously consented, and arranged for us to meditate a few mornings a week at his apartment, before I had to be at work.

We meditated to an intriguing tape of the Tibetan bells. They sounded more like hovering spaceships to me however, than bells. And I could feel their vibrations reverberating through me. I really resonated to them. They felt familiar. I had been told by one of the entities that speak through Kevin Ryerson that I was a Tibetan monk in a past life, but I still was weighing that possibility.

In one of my morning meditations with Santi, I quite lucidly saw two identical, clear crystal balls, skewered horizontally by a single beam of amber light. It was as if the spirit realm was communicating to me in symbols. The literal meaning behind the representations was not so important to me. What I responded to was, more the purity of the symbols. Supreme intelligence was disguised as something so clear and simple in these precious spheres. I could feel that. They were gifts. And wondrous to behold.

Santi was soon to be leaving for Australia for three months, to undergo rebirther training. So we planned to get together one last time, for dinner, before he left. We met at my house. As I recall, he came over in the late afternoon so that we could meditate before dinner.

Santi had been meditating for years, and with the assistance of George Daisly, had developed not only his psychic and intuitive abilities, but also a deep bond with the spirit realm. He conversed regularly with his own spirit guides and teachers, and was opening himself up further to trance channel.

We concluded our meditation and were leaving my room when Santi stopped, scrunched his face--suggesting that he was straining to hear something inaudible--and then abruptly halted the question on my lips. He then waved whatever he was listening to closer to his ear, stopped for a moment, and reported with a broad smile "You have a Dr. Chang working with you. He's here to help you with your writing."

"Oh, yeah?" I responded, nonplused.

Santi then went into an elaborate description of the gentleman. Flowing robe, Fu Manchu mustache, the whole bit. It's not that I didn't believe him, it's just that I still had trouble believing anything of this nature unless I had my own experiences of them. After all, that's how I started out in the first place. I set out to experience and obtain my own proof. And yes, by this time I had gotten plenty of proof. But that didn't mean I had to believe everything every psychic or entity channeled through a medium, had to tell me.

A month or so passed. I was meditating fairly regularly, and as usual, reading two or three metaphysical books at a time. One of my favorite things to do on weekends, was to go out by myself for breakfast, and bring some reading material to devour along with my meal.

On one such weekend, however, my timing was off a bit, and I found myself among a throng of equally starving diners waiting for tables. Luckily, the wait went fast, and soon there were only two or three of us left to be seated. To my left sat a woman in her early 30s. She was as fond of a morning read as I was, which was made apparent by the two volumes sitting atop her lap. I had just finished reading the top book, the title of which escapes me, and used my good experience with it as a conversation starter.

We continued conversing, and before we knew it, a table had been made available, which we quickly opted to share. We enthusiastically swapped book titles we'd enjoyed, the recent workshops we had found worthwhile, our experiences in general, and the psychic readings we had.

"I just came from a reading," she offered.

"Oh, really?" I inquired with interest, "With whom?"

"Her name is Bette Hanks, and she's been psychic all her life. Her parents were even into this stuff."

"Huh?" I interrupted quizzically, "I've never heard of her."

"That's because she's a little unconnected with the mainstream. But I felt that it was a very accurate reading, and believe me I've had a bunch of them, and this one was very right on--and she only charges $35!"

Hanks. That was Lincoln's mother's name, I thought.

I quickly copied down the phone number. It appealed to me that Bette wasn't on the "circuit" and that she had an impressive reputation. The fact that she charged such a reasonable fee was an added bonus. The question regarding money in exchange for psychic and spiritual services was certainly an open-ended one. I had heard both sides of the often-heated debate, and now was grateful to have found someone within my financial means. How accurate she would be, I knew not, but I was of the mind, that the cost of this service, was inconsequential in this regard. I still was so curious and intrigued about the channeling process, so I promptly called Bette right from the restaurant, and booked a reading with her for the next day.

Bette lived in one of the few parts of town that I was unfamiliar with. It was a retirement mobile home park of some kind. When she came to the door, I found a tall, jovial, English woman, who still retained the charming accent. We then settled into chairs in her modest living room. I guessed her to be in her early 60s.

Mediumship ran in Bette's family. A gifted sensitive herself, Bette was granted the privilege of witnessing her parents pass into spirit. And like Nora Grafton, another British sensitive, she saw and conversed with her family in spirit regularly. But rather than having entities speak through her, the way they do through such well known trance channels as Kevin Ryerson, Elwood Babbitt, and Verna Yater,

Bette would go into a trance and both retrieve information and deliver impressions from the spirit dimension.

According to Bette--now in trance, there was apparently a tall, wealthy Bostonian banker, placing huge, overstuffed bags of money at my feet. This was a nice switch from sloppily painted karmic messages and uninvited spirits broadcasting without permits --through my head.

"One of your teachers is here," Bette informed me, from deep trance.

"I believe his name is Chang," she paused. "Yes, a Dr. Chang."

Chang! Chang! Chang! The name clanged through my head like a freight train. How could this be? Wasn't this the same guide Santi had told me a month earlier was helping me with my writing?

Either this entity Chang got around, or I didn't know what to think. Not only had Santi and Bette not yet met, but Bette had never even heard of the institute.

Whenever I got positive proof in this way--that the spirit realm was indeed real--alive and kicking in fact, I still could not immediately overcome the initial shock of receiving the information. With this new news that perfectly corroborated the spirit relayed message through Santi, I was perked for the rest of this reading with Bette.

Unfortunately, however, I didn't remember much of what followed, and due to possible vibrational frequency interferences, tape recorders were prohibited.

But none of that mattered to me at the time, because with the sort of positive proof I had just received, I was too busy trying to figure out how to get in touch with this Dr. Chang.

Dr. Chang: "Phone home!"

Chapter 19

See Me, Touch Me, Heal Me

A friend had just received Reiki (ray-key), an ancient form of hands-on healing that originated in Tibet thousands of years ago, and offered to give me a treatment. Always curious of new means of healing, I accepted.

"Rei" means universal, and "ki" means energy. Through a series of attunements with a Reiki Master, one was able to channel this energy to oneself or others to heal on physical, emotional, mental, and spiritual levels.

The analogy was that the person giving the Reiki treatment was like jumper cables hooked up to universal energy. The person receiving the treatment was a battery in need of some juice.

When we began, I lay flat on my bed fully clothed. My friend placed his hands on different parts of my body that he explained were major energy centers. He held each position for a few minutes at a time.

The first thing I was aware of was heat coming from his hands. It didn't feel like your average everyday body heat, either. When I slowly turned over so he could work on the areas on my back, I went somewhere else. I was so relaxed from this energy boost that I must have gone out of my body, for when I came back he had already completed the last hand position (as they were called).

I felt so good, relaxed, and balanced that I signed up to get the Reiki attunements shortly thereafter.

In the course of the two-day workshop, we learned the hand positions and received the attunements from the Reiki Master. I really can't describe exactly how the attunements were done, as my eyes were closed for this ritual, but I did feel an energy coming into me.

For the remainder of the workshop, we gave one another treatments. We were given a handbook containing an A-to-Z index for specific treatments so we could spend extra time on troubled areas.

Shortly after I received Reiki I went to New York to visit my family. My sister, Anne Marie, had a sty that had been bothering her. So I looked up the hand positions and gave her a treatment. I was surprised to learn from her that by the next day the sty had all but vanished. She further mentioned that the sties she got usually took her two or three days to heal.

When I got back to California, a Reiki network had been set up on a regular basis so that those of us who wanted to exchange "hands-on," as the first level of Reiki was called (at the time there were three levels of Reiki available), could do so. Even though I was capable of administering a treatment to myself, it was always more pleasurable for me to receive from others.

What also was nice about these gatherings was that I could mingle with like-minded people and have an opportunity to make new friends.

Chapter 20

Baby Jane Meets Sweet Charlotte

It was becoming increasingly difficult to stabilize the house in which I then was living in terms of roommates. Either people would stay only for a short time or they were near psychotic. On one occasion, before ejecting a roommate who was in need of psychiatric help, I had a scary and at the same time profound experience.

One night three or four of us were talking in the kitchen. I merely stated my opinion on some matter to the young man in question, not knowing of his unbalanced state, and startlingly received a Kung Fu kick in my face. I was too shocked to move for a second; more shocked than hurt, however.

I certainly was not about to retaliate. So I found myself just looking at the guy, and within seconds he burst into tears and then began embracing me. On a deep level I knew something remarkable had taken place.

I was wondering if the universe was giving me another kick. I now was meditating and finding it nearly impossible to do so in my current surroundings. So with the good money I now was making I was determined to live alone again for a while.

A devastating fire had just finished blazing through nearby Ojai, and on the fourth of July, as I found myself in search of new living space, debris from the fire's aftermath rained on Santa Barbara.

The sky was a putrid gray-brown. The mercury had broken 90 degrees and was rising. The energy-zapping humidity added to the overall war-zone feel to this usually paradisaic beach town.

To make matters worse, my car was again in the shop, so I was on foot. My scratchy throat, which was further exacerbated by the smoky air, threatened me with the flu.

I walked the streets like a nomadic zombie, with my hands cupped around my throat in a Reiki position, repeating the affirmation "I am perfect health, I am perfect health..." while my eyes burned beneath my contact lenses.

It was as if the environment now was symbolically reflecting back to me my stifling living environment. They both were unbearable.

By this time I had arrived at an old apartment building. I slowly made my way up the flight of stairs to the available unit. I tried the door, and it opened.

The reflection of the light through the three windows on the far side of the room greeted me on the hardwood floor as I stepped into the otherwise empty room. I suddenly felt energized. I slid to the center of the room. I could see into the small compact kitchen and out the window above the bathtub in the postage-stamp-sized bathroom. There was even a tiny view of the mountains from the bathtub.

This was the place! I could feel it in my solar plexus. I ran into the kitchen and tested out the built-in table and bench set. I spilled myself halfway out the window to take in the view, where fragrant jacarandas blossomed below me.

I felt like I was in an apartment in New York or San Francisco in the 1930s. I could hear Charlie Parker in my head. Yes, I would take this apartment.

I went back home and collapsed. By the next morning my throat had healed and I was better. I guess the Reiki/affirmation combo had worked.

In about a week I was moved into my new home and alone at last!

The institute brought Kevin Ryerson back for another series of evening workshops. Based on my good experience with his previous class, I took it.

At the end of Ryerson's classes he usually channels for about an hour, giving the group an opportunity to pose questions of spirit. Unlike my other encounters at trance channeling demonstrations, tonight I was more vocal. I had had an incredibly vivid dream that I wanted clarified. I did have some tools at my disposal for dream deciphering, but it always was nice to get a second opinion--especially from spirit. So I took advantage of the opportunity.

When the entity John, from biblical times, came through, I told him and the group present of my dream.

What I immediately noticed about this dream was the lighting. It was like an exquisite art film lit in burnt oranges. All of the characters had a coppery hue to them as well. It was quite stunning to look at.

Shimmering. The action took place on a farm, though I know not where. The other thing about the dream was that, like a film, I was observing it but not participating in it.

The plot line was so intricate and yet cohesive, unlike most random rambling dreams, which led me to believe that this was perhaps a past-life flashback. I had learned that this was one of the possibilities of what we could experiences when we closed our eyes at night to sleep. I imagined that from this entity's perspective point, he might be able to shine some new light on it.

The plot revolved around a love triangle: a farmer and two women who I believe were sisters. One of the two was blind and crippled and confined to a wheelchair. The farmer was having an affair with the other sister and planning to marry her soon.

When the crippled sister, a very manipulative woman, got wind of the upcoming marriage in a private moment with the farmer, she feigned self-pity and remorse in hopes of swaying his affections. She succeeded, and the farmer now promised to marry her instead.

The plot thickened when the eavesdropping crippled sister overheard the farmer confide to the other sister that he gave into the crippled woman and promised to marry her because he felt sorry for her. He now knew that he would soon be forced to tell the cripple his true intentions: to marry her sister as originally planned.

Upon receiving this information from this clandestine little meeting, the crippled woman deliberately turned toward an imaginary camera with a glint in her eye and a sinister smile. She now would plot to kill her sister. *Shades of Sweet Charlotte meets Baby Jane--in a past life!*

Then I woke up.

After finishing my account of the dream, I was expecting the ancient entity to verify the past life, elucidate on the fine points, and relate the implications on this life. But this did not occur. Instead the entity who walked for a time with Jesus bid farewell to allow another entity to handle the question.

Tom McPherson, the Irish rogue, popped in and promptly asked me to repeat the dream to him. After doing so, he then explained that the dream was more symbolic than past-life material and that I had placed myself outside of the dream so that I could view different aspects of myself objectively.

The symbolism had to do with my androgyny--the male and female inner parts of me. Tom guessed that in the last year I had become more comfortable with the female part of myself--the spiritual, intuitive side. This, of course, was quite true.

The female part of me was developing to the point that it could be intuitive and insightful, symbolized by the healthy sister. But it also could be overly analytical, irritable, and short-tempered at times, too. This was the "blind" or "crippled" side that was symbolized by the crippled sister.

Tom further suggested that the crippling side, the critical or irritable side of my ego, might be holding me back from the progress I had made so far spiritually by preventing the merger of the inner male and female--the left and right sides of my brain.

The explanation made a lot of sense to me. I had been very pragmatic in my search for truth so far, and still remained somewhat skeptical at times. Maybe the dream had been a message for me to lighten up a little, to trust more. In so doing I would open further.

When I got home from the workshop, I felt a presence in the room. It was playful. Having just spent some time with the entities that came through Ryerson, I suspected that it was McPherson, the Irish rouge. I felt like I was supposed to do something, only I didn't know what.

Just for the fun of it, I laid down on my bed and arranged a few crystals on my body at certain chakra points. I then began to meditate. I was hoping that this might amplify the transmission as I had read certain crystals could do, and maybe find out what McPherson wanted of me if in fact it was him present.

As I relaxed into meditation I remembered a dream from the previous night. In this dream a friend had told me that she had found out that her husband had been having little affairs behind her back. I had known this to be the case in the waking reality and told her so.

"Why didn't you tell me sooner if you knew?" she pleaded.

I explained to her that I didn't feel that it was right for me to intrude. Since she had found out anyway, things unfolded as they were supposed to without me having to interfere.

When I finished my quasi-meditation, I felt that I was supposed to call my friend from the dream. It seemed silly to me. But then again lots of things had felt silly to me. So I went ahead and dialed the number that I hadn't called in many months.

My friend wasn't home, her husband explained. They were separated!

I almost laughed, but quickly regained my composure and explained to him why I really had called. I told him of my dream minus the details about his affairs.

Excited with this new bit of proof spurned from another precognitive dream, I lightheadedly hung up the phone.

Chapter 21

Creativity and Responsibility

As I was moving forward on my path/adventure, I spent more time with new friends Nancy and Jane. Nancy was the woman who had done my resume that I felt helped me to land the new job. Jane was the woman who worked with me at the new company with whom I began taking spiritual classes.

When the thought finally came to me, I had to marvel at winning the computer job without agency intervention or agency fee and that I had this new good friend in Nancy as a by-product of the original computer position experience. I never did find out if my present employer had placed the job order with the agency, though.

While we didn't take classes together, Nancy and I would talk nonstop of what we were learning spiritually when we would get together. We swapped books and we shared our adventures in and out of the dream state.

Because we worked together, Jane and I ate lunch together frequently and shared bits from the two and three books we both usually read at a time. We would discuss the work of Edgar Cayce, perhaps the most consistent, well-documented, and renowned trance medium in the world.

We'd look at our lives and speculate what our current karma might be.

We were serious searchers. We both felt that we were getting some answers. That's what made it all so exciting!

Nancy and Jane were the beginning of my spiritual support group. I told them about each other over the past six months, but never had thought to have them meet. Jane recently was married, so I didn't see her too much outside of work, lunch, or the classes we took together.

One day at work I was on the phone talking with Nancy, and I somehow mentioned Jane's husband's name. Since it was a rather unusual name, Nancy stopped for a moment and took note.

"Wait a minute," she said as she proceeded to describe both Jane and her husband, Cleaver.

"But how do you know them?" I asked, a little puzzled.

"They live downstairs from me."

"They do?" I said in disbelief.

"Cleaver's parents own the building and rented the apartment to me, and there were fifty other applicants!"

I again found it strange how I was to meet these two women who knew each other, at about the same time, and with both of them heavily intrigued with metaphysics/spirituality--in a town of almost 150,000 people. It was uncanny.

This, coupled with all that was happening to me, was indeed synchronistic. Whoever was responsible for this impeccable sleight of hand was to be commended. They certainly had me going.

As I've mentioned earlier, when I got "hooked" on my spiritual journey/adventure, music got put on hold. This was very different for me. I had written more than 100 songs over the past twenty years, something I never planned to do. Maybe I was channeling these songs, as I started writing music without lessons. But now I had stopped.

I was absorbed in learning about myself, my purpose, and my relation to the world. But this would not be an end in itself, or would it? It certainly felt like it could be. Since being in touch with one's feelings was at the crux of much of metaphysics, I was now following my feelings.

Part of the reason that I think I temporarily abandoned music had to do with responsibility. I had learned that we had the power to manifest whatever it was we desired, that thoughts and words were things, and that the thoughts we held consciously and unconsciously propelled us to our individual and collective destinies.

We all were little computers that from youth had been shaped to a large extent by the software we were fed by parents, teachers, the media, and society at large.

When I thought about it, there was a lot of negativity going out on the airwaves. I wasn't judging it as right or wrong, it just seemed that if a song had a nifty little groove and punched lyrics like "kill, kill, kill...", or a song that drove the message into one's head that crying or showing one's feelings was unacceptable behavior, we could be negatively affected by them in some way.

Many of the songs I had written were different variations of rock music with what I thought were witty lyrics. I did write a mixed bag. But when I looked at some of the material, I wasn't so sure that I would want these messages going out.

At the time I wrote some of these songs, I actually was processing emotionally and the songs were the catharsis. Sometimes the songs could get ugly.

I realized that this was how art was, in some instances, created and that there really wasn't any judgment attached to it. It's just that in playing some of these songs long after they had been written, I usually felt emotionally divorced from them and performed them from a total ego mode. What was the point?

They had been useful to me emotionally and artistically. But if I were lucky enough to land a record deal, couldn't I just as easily promote more of the inspirational songs I had written instead?

Now I was looking at my shadow self and my light self. They were both valid parts of me that deserved equal time. But did that mean I broadcast both parts to an impressionable world that may misinterpret me?

I didn't have the total answer, and for the moment it didn't matter. I was still in search of other things.

Chapter 22

All Is Revealed in the Dream

"For God speaketh once,
yea twice, though man
regardeth it not. In a dream,
in a vision of the night, when deep
sleep falleth upon man, in slumberings
upon his bed; then he openeth the ears of
men, and sealeth their instruction."

--Job 33:14-16

So much of what I had experienced had occurred in dream states: the out-of-body episodes in my bedroom; the vestitures dream with Salvador Dali; the alpha state experiences with the business card and the golden temple; the "enchanted evening" breaking the time warp; and the direct spirit transmission, unbeknownst to the FCC, through the back of my head.

I also had done a lot of dream work in Verna Yater's class at the Spiritual Sciences Institute. In Verna's insightful class I learned that there are a wide variety of possible experiences one could expect in the dream state. There were meetings that took place with one's spirit guides and teachers. There were precognitive dreams and prophetic dreams. There were rich, multilayered dreams comprised of custom-made symbols for individual interpretation, as opposed to stereotypical dream symbols such as going into a tunnel being synonymous with sex or death, as some dream books profess.

There were past-life flashes and future-life flashes. There were out-of-body experiences and there were lucid dreams.

There are, of course, other probable experiences that transpire when we sleep, such as abduction by aliens and so on.

But I still was evaluating the previously mentioned possibilities before taking on aliens--or being taken by them.

Remembering Dreams

The first step in working with dreams is being able to remember them. The best way to remember one's dreams is to set an intention to do so before drifting into sleep. The intention plants a seed in the subconscious.

It also is advisable to have either a pad and pen or a tape recorder accessible by one's bedside, along with a dim lamp. Upon waking in the middle of the night, one usually can remember the last dream dreamt. Be careful to keep movement to a minimum as this disturbs the dream engrams--the last frames of a given dream.

It especially is important to write down dreams that are powerful enough to wake us. These dreams usually hold many clues and messages.

Before getting out of bed in the morning, more dreams can be added to the list. I've found it helpful to re-read the dreams from the middle of the night, because in so doing I usually remember more dreams and details that I had missed writing down previously.

Working with Dreams

There are many ways of working with dreams. In working with the symbolic variety of dreams in Verna Yater's class, I found a few simple yet quite revealing techniques. Of course, the more one works with dreams, other techniques for dream interpretation may be discovered.

Begin by reliving the dream. Write it on paper and give as much detail as possible. Include your feelings at each changing interval in the dream. Next, comprise a list of all of the symbols. Go back over the list and pick out the three or four most important symbols. A good way to test the importance of a symbol is to close your eyes and feel the symbol. The symbols with the most charge--the ones that press a button in us one way or another--usually are the ones with which to work.

After you have your symbols, write down the first symbol on a sheet of paper. Divide the page into two columns below the symbol. (I usually keep a spiral notebook exclusively for working with dreams so I can date the dreams and refer back to them.)

For the rest of the exercise, you can work with either a partner or by yourself. Working with a partner initially is beneficial because it gives you the opportunity to freely associate, which is crucial to the exercise. Later, after you've become more adept in working with your dreams, you can get good results by working alone.

If you're working with a partner, pick a specific dream and then the first symbol from your list of symbols from that dream. Your partner then will rapidly and repeatedly ask you what you like about the symbol. Stick with your first impressions. Freely associate rather than think your responses; you will have many.

As you respond, your partner will transcribe your responses in the first column. Work quickly and don't be afraid to repeat a response if it keeps coming up, it is undoubtedly an important clue. You should work for at least five minutes on each symbol. You'll be surprised at how much information you'll gather.

When you've exhausted what you liked about the symbol, repeat the procedure with what you did *not* like about the symbol. Your partner then will enter these responses in the remaining column.

After you've finished the first symbol, do the remaining two or three symbols from the dream on which you are working. Only work on one dream at a time or you'll get confused.

When you've finished with your likes and dislikes of each symbol, your partner then will read back to you what you liked about the symbol. From this list pick the one response that you resonated to most, and your partner will circle it. Repeat this procedure with the most striking dislike of the symbol, and again your partner will circle the response. Then do this for the remaining symbols.

When you have finished, list the symbols with the circled responses on a separate sheet of paper. In so doing you probably will begin to see some correlations and gain some clarity about the dream.

Frequently, when I've done two or more dreams from the same chosen night, with two or three symbols from each dream, I see that the message that I got was the same in all of my dreams for that night. But experiment for yourself.

If one of the symbols still puzzles you, take a clean sheet of paper and draw the symbol on the entire sheet. If you want to get creative with crayons, inks, paint, or another media, feel free to do so, as this may bring you closer to understanding the significance of the symbol.

Become the symbol by holding the sheet of paper with the symbol in front of your face like a mask. To assist you in this your partner now will ask you (as the symbol) a series of questions beginning with the words who, what, when, or where. Your partner can ask anything of you with the exception of a "why" question. For example, if the symbol were a door, your partner may ask, "What does it feel like to be a door? "Where do you live, door?" "When were you born, door?" Your partner will record your replies.

This new information and experience, coupled with the previous exercise, usually is quite effective in unravelling dreams. As you work more creatively with your dreams, you not only will begin to see which dreams were symbolic, past-life flashes, meetings with your guides, or other possible experiences; but you also will strengthen your relationship with your guides and teachers and gain enormous self-clarity.

As I've mentioned earlier in this text, the conscious state is as much of a dream as the dreams we experience in our sleep. Since this is the case, the little episodes that weave together to form the fabric of our lives then can be viewed as dreams as well, complete with symbols.

Since these experiences also are dreams, we can work with the symbols that appear in our everyday lives in the previously mentioned ways as well. For example, if we get a flat tire, this becomes a symbol we may want to work on.

This concept of being able to work on symbols in our awake state as if they were sleep-state dream symbols is further reinforced by synchronicity, the theory that there are no accidents or coincidences.

Lucid Dreams

One of the experiences occurring in the dream state that most intrigued me was the lucid dream. This is the experience of knowing one is dreaming and feeling as if the dream is real and actually happening as if you are awake.

I would have these experiences from time to time, but it was always spontaneous.

In one such dream I remember being chased down the street on which I grew up. As I ran down the street, the dream became lucid in front of my house. Having the awareness that I was dreaming, I then told myself, "Well, if this is a dream, then I can fly." So I did.

Through the glowing chartreuse branches of a maple tree made transparent by the nearby street lamp, I quickly ascended and left my would-be captors to clutch at fistfuls of air on the pavement below.

Later I would experience the spirit communication broadcast lucidly, as well as my not so "enchanted evening."

I found these experiences and others that I had had thrilling. But as I've said, since these lucid dreams were involuntary, I never knew when I could expect them.

When shopping at my favorite bookstore in Santa Barbara, I accidentally happened upon the almost hidden magazine room, a feature of the store that unfortunately had eluded me for months. Not only did I discover the expansive magazine stand, but I soon found, for the first time, intriguing and informative new age/metaphysical/spiritual magazines. And there were lots of them!

There was *Magical Blend*, *New Age*, *Life Times* (published by Santa Barbara friends Jack and Cai Underhill), *The Yoga Journal* and *The Shaman's Drum* to name a few.

I grabbed a magazine that had an article on lucid dreams. It really was an excerpt from Stephen LaBerge's visionary work *Lucid Dreaming*. The fascination and passion that the article ignited in me propelled me to the cashier counter to order the store's first copy. I couldn't wait to get my hands on this book.

When the LaBerge book arrived, I began devouring it. As I did with the Monroe book, I cheated and skipped to the "how-to" section of this book on lucid dreaming.

I loved this type of dream. They always were so magical. If I could have them at will, then going to sleep at night could promise to be one of the most pleasurable and entertaining of experiences, putting the other medias to shame.

There were many different methods outlined in the LaBerge book for achieving the lucid state in the dream state. Some were taken from ancient yogic traditions, and some LaBerge invented himself. I opted for one of LaBerge's methods, which also seemed to me to be the most simple.

To begin with it is helpful to set an intention at some point in the day to have a lucid dream that night, and to remind oneself in the course of the day of that intention.

Before closing one's eyes for the night, the next step is to again reaffirm the intention to have a lucid dream. While still awake but with eyes closed, repeat, "One, I'm dreaming, two, I'm dreaming..." until dreaming occurs.

If one is lucky enough to enter into a lucid dream at this point, the lucidity probably will not last for very long due to technicalities having to do with rapid eye movement (REM).

In the course of the night, possibly between 3 and 5 in the morning, repeat the "One, I'm dreaming..." procedure upon waking. My experience has been that with the repetition of this phrase at this time of night, lucidity in the dream state results almost immediately and can be extended for quite a long period of time. LaBerge further mentions that from his personal experience, naps in the late afternoon provide a climate for lucid dreaming six times greater than at night.

When I thought about it, I remembered that my lucid experiences of swooping into the gold-inlaid temple and with the hand holding the mysterious business card took place during my late afternoon naps. While those occurrences were involuntary, like my lucid dream of being chased, I now decided to follow the guidance of the LaBerge book to deliberately experiences lucid dreams.

Unfortunately, I wasn't as lucky as I had been with the Monroe book in quickly achieving an out-of-body state. As I was to learn, lucid dreaming took some discipline, patience, and work!

I don't know how long it took me to successfully have a lucid dream, but it was at least a few weeks after religiously practicing LaBerge's technique.

What follows are a series of my most memorable lucid dreams.

The First Dream

I was in New York City, although I don't know exactly where. There was a light grey stone building--actually a small cluster of them. The tallest was two or three stories high. The impression I got was that the main building was a church of some kind. In front of the building a group of eight or ten people had congregated.

At first I simply surveyed the scene.Then the dream became lucid. I was surprised! Like a kid let loose in a candy store, I didn't know where to begin.

In my excited state, I felt I had to share this experience with someone. So I exuberantly rushed over to the group and interrupted their conversation by exclaiming, "You're all in a dream that I'm having right now!"

I couldn't wait for their response. But there was none. They simply turned to me for a brief moment and then resumed their previous posture as if I didn't exist. I was stunned.

This is incredible, I thought. Here I was, for the first time successfully and deliberately achieving lucidity in the dream state, and alerting these inhabitants of my dream landscape of this fact, and there response was *no* response. It was like being in an episode of the old, enigmatic television show, "The Prisoner."

I wasn't about to let this experience be wasted, so I darted away from them in a mad frenzy. I felt as though the dream would end if I didn't do something soon.

I remembered from the LaBerge book that in one of Carlos Castaneda's *Don Juan* books, being able to see one's hand in the dream state could bring about or stabilize the lucid state. So I immediately anchored my right hand onto the tree in front of myself and desperately focused my concentration on the back side of my hand.

I saw these swirling paisley patterns of energy dance within the confines of my hand, so as not to spill out onto the tree. I felt my focus being pulled, however. The more I stared into these mesmerizing designs, the larger they became. They threatened to swallow me in the process. In an effort to brake free from the strong hold of this unnamed energy, and to remain lucid, I quickly flipped my hand over in hopes of breaking the spell.

Not only was I successful in my fight, but I now could miraculously see--in complete detail--the fingerprint of my index finger! I was amazed.

With this, the peak of my monumental experience, the lucidity dissolved and I lapsed into normal dreaming.

The Second Dream

Rain was pouring down as I went running down a street. For some reason I felt so alone that the pain ached inside and outside of me, gnawing at my core.

In the very next moment I had a brief flash of something that filled me with supreme joy. I could feel white light radiating from my solar plexus in all directions.

I now was running with a group of young people, hippie types in their early to mid-20s. I knew that these people were the cause of my joy. It was as if I had forgotten that I had these beautiful friends in my life, and in my moment of need they suddenly materialized to remind me of this. Only the *me* in this dream didn't know who they were. I didn't recognize anyone. I only knew--because I had felt it-- that these were precious people to me and that I was loved.

We trampled into a house like a herd of cattle and took refuge from the rain. I stayed in the living room, but the rest of the group whooshed past me like a team of marathon runners. Sprinting down a short, narrow hallway, they abruptly cut to the left and were gone. A young woman and I remained in the living room in their wake.

I watched as this hippie girl picked up an infant from out of a shoe box on the floor by the hallway. I thought to myself, *How can she be so irresponsible as to leave her baby alone with no one to attend to it?*

As this thought left me, the girl dropped the baby back into the box as though it was a football! This outrageous behavior shocked me to say the least. But what really shocked me occurred when the girl nonchalantly threw a pair of large metal scissors into the box before scooting down the hallway to join the others!

I immediately went over to rescue the baby. Expecting to find blood from the scissors, I scooped the baby into my arms to find that it had changed. It clearly had transformed from a real baby into one made of "Play-Doh." Now I was confused.

But then it hit me. *This baby was real a few seconds ago, and now it's made of "Play-Doh"?* I quizzically thought to myself. This was no sleight of hand! This was a dream! I now was blissfully lucid thanks to this macabre little event, and I was excited! It was another opportunity--but for what I did not know. But I did know one thing: I had to work fast!

I excitedly rounded the corner down the hallway. In my haste, I misjudged the doorway to what turned out to be the kitchen and scraped my left shoulder on the door frame.

"Hey, you guys! Come here!" I yelled out.

But remembering the nonplussed reaction I received from the people in front of the church in my other lucid experience, I eased up in my approach.

"Now I know what I'm about to tell you is a little strange, but please listen to me."

They all stopped what they were doing, faced me, and intently listened.

"Something's definitely going on. This has happened to me before. I need you all to listen carefully and to focus." I paused, still in full lucidity.

"You're all in a dream I'm having right now," I began.

Unlike my previous similar dream, they not only comprehended what I was saying, but they also were touched. An aura of reverence pervaded. No one spoke. They simply held their concentration. I could feel the intensity of all of their eyes now on me as they awaited further instruction.

"I think it would be good if we formed a circle and joined hands."

We accomplished this in seconds. I was shocked. They were really with me on this! The energy was so concentrated that the lucidity somehow increased. I was spellbound.

I looked across the room and could feel a deep bond with the young man across the circle. His imploring eyes were in earnest. He also knew that something quite profound was occurring. But for the moment I was lost. I could float a little in my consciousness since the group's energy was so powerfully holding the dream lucid.

Then I had a flash.

"I know! Let's all call one another tomorrow on the phone!"

I remember asking one of the women what her phone number was so that all of us could call her the next day, but I only got the first three digits when the lucidity began to wan. Like a wave, the lucidity rose and fell around the circle, until like in an atom smasher, each particle of consciousness fell apart and I awoke.

Hours later, in the morning light, I lay mesmerized in my bed with what had happened. I had come so close to something. I absolutely knew that what had occurred was real and I wondered what was going on in the minds of those who for such a brief time had shared with me something so special. I wondered if they, too, felt the wonder, bewilderment, and frustration of not being able to contact the other dream participants as I had.

I resolved now that should I luck out and again be in such a situation, it would be *my* phone number everyone would call. At least that was a number I could remember.

The Third Dream

A meeting was about to take place. The meeting room was a professional environment with white walls, a shiny white, tiled floor, and fluorescent lighting that made the room seem to vibrate.

A group of men and women in uniforms featuring blue blazers and grey slacks came rushing in with headsets dangling from their heads, leading me to speculate that they were from a phone company of some kind.

I was in the process of orienting myself in this frenetic scene when the dream went lucid. Unlike the magical experience with my hippie friends, I wasn't quite sure how the news would be received when I would again alert my fellow dream participants of the reality that now was transpiring.

When I finally did reveal what I was experiencing to this group, the reaction was different from both the stony church people and from my young hippie friends.

They laughed at me when I told them they were all in a dream I now was having! I felt like Jimmy Stewart in *Harvey*. Only I now was the six-foot rabbit no one wanted to believe was there!

I had to think fast while they still surrounded me. Somehow, group energy helped to hold the lucidity, as in the experience with my hippie friends.

I had done improvisation before in comedy groups, but this exercise was especially challenging. Not only did I need to come up with something that would prove that what I was saying was true, but I also had the additional challenge of being the sole player in this "improv" and had the pressure of succeeding before the lucid state dissolved. I never knew when that would be.

Standing in the center of this group of what looked like deranged air traffic controllers with their headsets wildly flailing, I quickly said, "I know! Pick me up! If this is a dream, I should be very light."

Humoring me, they obliged by lifting my body into the air. They seemed to struggle, but I assumed they were feigning the strain to prove me wrong.

"Well? Tell me!"

"You're as heavy as a cow!" one of them yelled as they almost immediately dropped me back to the floor with a thud. The funny thing was that I felt heavy to myself as well.

They continued milling around and joking in the time they had before the meeting was to begin. I then had the feeling, and I don't quite remember what triggered it, that it no longer was 1989 (the year in which I had this particular dream).

"What year is it?" I demanded to know.

"What do you think!" one of them caustically replied.

"I don't know."

Finally, "Two," came the exasperated response.

"Two? Two what?"

"What do you think?"

"2000?" I guessed.

"No--20,000," someone joked amid the group laughter.

I couldn't believe it! I was lucid in my "dream" and in the future! I couldn't think straight. I had a million questions. Now it didn't seem so important to convince these people of my lucidity; I had another mystery to explore.

"Is there a Democrat in the White House?" I found myself asking.

When this was affirmed I asked for the name of the new president. But this part was a little jumbled in my memory the next morning when I relived the experience.

There were three names that came to mind in different combinations. One was Arthur Sinclair. Another was Arthur Fairchild. The third was Fairchild Sinclair. The last one, Fairchild Sinclair, is the one that felt right. But Arthur Sinclair sounded more plausible. I couldn't be sure. But I added it to my list of projects to research.

The lucidity started to fade at this point in my questioning. I begged the group to help hold the focus by threatening to disappear and wake up. But their pervading flippancy caused this very thing to occur.

The Fourth Dream

I was in a familiar restaurant, sitting at a table with a man and a woman that I did not know. On the table there was a map that looked like a map of the world. The map took up the entire surface of the table top. The man was talking to the woman about the map. At this point the dream became lucid.

The man was sitting across from me, and he now was including me in the conversation. He had a presumptuous, self-important, devilish manner about him that I immediately disliked.

"Oh, he's a very good actor," he whispered to the woman while staring at me, a smirk on his high-cheekboned face. I knew he was referring to me, only I did not know this man and wondered when, if ever, he had seen me act.

"Wait a minute," I deliberately interrupted, starting to feel a little suspicious. Placing equal emphasis on each word, I asked this stranger, "Who...are...you?"

"Oh, you can call me..." he paused, "Tim." He replied with a flourish and a half-cocked smile on his lizardlike lips that smacked of self-satisfaction.

The woman simply observed the entire event and said nothing.

"No," I paused. "Who are you--really?" I demanded to know, feeling slightly angry at his arrogance.

He unflinchingly stared back at me across the table as the dream's lucidity increased. The dream had become clearer than clear. Suddenly I could pick out every detail on this enigmatic, haughty gentleman's face. What wasn't so clear was this individual's identity.

Feeling an undercurrent of fear slowly rising in my solar plexus, I then remembered something. If one encounters what one thinks is a dark energy--a demonic energy--you're to ask, "Are you of the light?" and the entity knows it must answer.

With fear now overriding my anger, I made my request.

"Are you of the light?" I demanded, holding intense eye contact.

Then something remarkable occurred.

With the utterance of my words, he instantly backed away at terrific speed, creating a blur of his image in each of some fifty frames of film extending backwards for ten yards and then on into infinity.

Like a special effect from a horror film, I could see him shrinking away in the blur of each frame. It was as if a powerful force from behind his chair were pulling him to another dimension. The next second he was gone.

The Fifth Dream

I was in the bedroom of my youth, standing by the window and looking out into the night. Someone grabbed me from behind in a bear hug that threatened to squeeze all the life out of me. Petrified from the shock of this attack and unable to move, I closed my eyes as a form of escape.

Finally I asked, "Who is it?"

"Your friend," came the sinister reply.

"But who?" I again asked, stuttering slightly.

"Tim."

I was feeling a strange mixture of fear and trust. I sensed evil and danger, but still somehow trusted.

The dream had a tinge of lucidity to it that made it all the more scary. But since my eyes were closed, it was difficult to gauge just how lucid it was, and at that point I couldn't have cared less. I just wanted out of this situation!

He then slowly turned around, still strongly holding me. I was feeling a mixture of fear and trust but kept my eyes closed. With my eyes closed I visualized white light and spread it all over him and the room. Who knew what else lurked where?

At the next moment we were on the top of a flight of stairs that led down to the second floor. Since nothing terrible had happened, I decided to slowly open my eyes. He looked different from our last encounter in the restaurant.

I somehow surrendered to this dark force. At once he evaporated into the air and I was free.

When I woke I felt a strange tingling intermittently throughout my body. I felt totally and completely free.

All lucid dreams can be evaluated like symbolic dreams. I found these last two dreams particularly symbolic.

I realized that the entity I had encountered was my shadow--the part of ourselves we don't like. This is the part we don't even like to admit exists, and as such unconsciously project onto others.

When I thought about my descriptions of the enigmatic man in the fourth dream, I had to admit these were elements of myself. The main difference between the two dreams was that in the first dream with my shadow in the restaurant, I viewed this entity as other than myself and sent it on its way, while in the second dream a real healing occurred by surrendering to the dark side of myself.

While I personally found the experience of lucid dreaming fun, thrilling, and an adventure in consciousness, according to the LaBerge book there were other more practical applications of lucid dreaming such as anxiety reduction, decision making, creative problem solving, and wish fulfillment to name a few.

As I experimented more with lucid dreaming, I developed another theory about them: Our subconscious minds to a large extent ran our lives. As such our subconscious minds drew us to people and situations it desired for us to experience. Through hypnosis, subliminal tapes (another form of hypnosis), and other methods, people tried to reprogram their subconscious minds to be able to manifest what they consciously wanted for themselves or wanted to rid themselves of, such as destructive habits like smoking.

It then occurred to me that we have the most direct accessibility to our subconscious minds in the dream state. Taken a step further, would it then not be possible to reprogram our "computers"--our subconscious minds--more effectively in the lucid state, when we have control over our dream landscapes?

Since I knew it was possible to control the dream when lucid, would we not then out-picture in our physical lives that which we consciously programmed into our subconscious minds when lucid dreaming?

It made sense to me, so this became the next thing with which I began experimenting. It was a slow process, however, since I did not dream lucidly every night. Time passed as I continued my experimentation. Then something else occurred to me.

If our subconscious always is present with us, and awake-state dream and sleep-state dreams basically were the same, why did I have to wait until my sleep time to do this work? With this in mind I then began working with affirmations.

Chapter 23

Yes I Can

Affirmations are positive statements describing what we want to bring into our lives. One such affirmation could be used to cultivate an attribute we lack, for example "I am an infinitely loving person." Maybe the affirmation is used to bring material objects one's way ("Endless money is flowing to me **now**!"), or to rid oneself of unwanted and undeserved emotions. For instance, if one feels guilty about something yet knows that they are innocent, the affirmation might be "I am totally innocent of any wrongdoing."

Affirmations also can be employed to bring relationships of all kinds into one's life, for example "I now have a meaningful, growth-oriented relationship with the partner of my divine selection." The possibility for affirmations is endless.

The necessary ingredients of an affirmation, however, are to always phrase the affirmation in the present and to always use a positive expression. For instance, if someone feels as though he is a failure, he would not phrase the affirmation "I am no longer a failure." Instead, he might say, "I now am successful." You do not necessarily have to believe the affirmation in order to work with it.

Following are some simple ways to work with affirmations. It is best to work with only two or three affirmations at a time. You can work with them either by writing them down or by recording them on a tape deck.

To begin with, pick your first affirmation. Make sure it is set in the present and that all of the words are positive. Be as specific as possible, however, because I've learned that it's best to keep one's options open. For instance, if you are working with an employment affirmation, you can mention a specific job opportunity that you are interested in, but simply add, "...or the job that will serve my highest good."

Generality is best in relationships as well. Say, "I now have a multitude of loving and supportive friends who accept me," or "I now have a loving, growth-oriented partnership with the mate of my divine selection."

If you are writing your affirmations down on paper, write them 20 times two or three times a day. Writing them in the morning helps set the mood for the day, and writing them just before bedtime plants some potent positive seeds into the highly programmable subconscious.

When you begin writing the first affirmation and doubts pop up, as they tend to do, acknowledge the doubt by writing down your feelings toward the affirmation on the line beneath the affirmation. We are all complex people with many mixed emotions or voices inside of us, and it helps to both integrate the voice and bring the affirmation into fruition by honoring these voices when they speak to us.

After you have written down the doubtful, negative, and possibly angry voice responses, continue writing your affirmation until you've written it 20 times. Then go to the other affirmations on which you plan to work.

When working with a tape recorder, record each affirmation ten to 20 times and play the tape at least two or three times a day, repeating the affirmation along with the tape. I have found this to work well for me. When your doubts come up, stop the tape and speak your doubts. Then play the affirmation until your doubts subside.

I like this method because I often am in my car and can listen to my affirmations frequently. It also helps keep my mind off of the traffic. Sometimes I even make up little melodies to go along with the affirmation, and I sing them. This I feel really helps lodge new positive ideas into the subconscious.

Whichever method you use, repeat these procedures for ten consecutive days per affirmation. When you've completed a ten-day interval, you can pick new affirmations or continue with some you are currently working with. But then let them go.

After a few months, if you still have not achieved the desired condition or situation, you may want to return to that affirmation. You may find that you had denied some of your feelings, your doubts, and that this got in the way of manifesting.

One last word on affirmations. Keep your affirmations to yourself! Sometimes people--friends, family, or loved ones--don't understand affirmations or believe that they work. This unnecessary negativity can be a strain and can be counterproductive to your good intentions. Only share your affirmations with those you know will support you.

For more information on affirmations, I highly recommend *I Deserve Love* by Sondra Ray and Florence Scovel Shinn's inspirational *The Game of Life and How to Play It*.

Chapter 24

Astrology: Blueprint for Transcendence

As I was exploring different areas of metaphysics and spirituality, I met someone who was very involved with astrology. He was a wealth of information on the subject and recommended many insightful books to me.

Years earlier I had my chart done, at a time when some friends and I used to throw the I Ching, the Chinese system of divination. I never took the I Ching or astrology that seriously then, but now that I had proof that reincarnation was a fact and that the spirit realm was real, I pursued astrology further.

I always had liked my sign, Aquarius, and could relate to the symbolism of the water bearer pouring the healing element of water into a world in much need of harmony, understanding, sympathy, and trust--as the popular song of the same name intoned.

Even as a child of four or five, I felt as though I was part of a bigger picture. One of my favorite books at the time was the Golden Book where a brother and sister visited other children from all over the world.

At that time I had had no experience with any race other than my own, yet I felt a camaraderie with these children of different nationalities in exotic costumes. Somehow they were familiar to me.

Since astrology is as complex and multilayered as any individual it professes to be able to decipher, I will limit my discussion to what astrology confirmed or reinforced for me (in terms of what I already knew about myself) and present the karmic aspects and transformational opportunities available in one's chart to balance karma.

So as not to lose sight of the main ideas I wish to get across, I will simplify as best as I can the sometimes confusing astrological buzz words that tend to alienate many (myself included at one point) from the promise astrology offers. These words and concepts are necessary to the understanding of oneself through astrology.

For those who would like to explore astrology further, I've included a bibliography in the form of recommended reading in the back of the book.

Knowing one's time, place, and date of birth, one can easily and inexpensively procure their birth chart from one of many computerized astrological services. With this information and the resources I've recommended, one can at least read up on the karmic potentials and see if this information is useful. For a more complete astrological reading, there are many fine astrologers available.

Contrary to popular belief, one is not automatically one's sun sign. In her in-depth book *Relating*, prominent British psychotherapist and astrologer Liz Greene says that the sun "...reflects the individual's urge to become himself...the urge for self-expression, self-realisation." The sun "...is a symbol of the ego...."

> Those qualities which the individual can potentially actualise in consciousness...are symbolised by the sign in which the sun is placed at birth.
>
> Your sun sign does not make you anything...it symbolises those energies, that particular myth [myths underscore each of the twelve zodiac signs], of which you are trying to learn how to become conscious, and trying to express in a creative way.

In my case, "...the Aquarius must learn to become conscious of the group life of which he is part, so that he can offer his share in the growth of collective consciousness."

In looking at one's chart you will notice that it is a circle divided into what looks like twelve pieces of a pie. Each pie piece is called a house. Noted astrologer Stephen Arroyo describes the houses as "fields of experience," with each house correlating to one of the 12 signs.

The first thing that I noticed about my chart that made a lot of sense to me was that the sun and the constellation (zodiac sign) of Aquarius were in the Fifth House at my time of birth. This house is associated with the sign Leo, meaning that the field of experiences would be Leonine in nature. Leonine characteristics have to do with creativity, play, and children (either actual or symbolic children, such as what one creates or holds dear to them), among other things.

If the sun had to do with ego and self-actualization, then in my case, in order to self-actualize I would do so through creativity since my sun occupies the Fifth House. Since the Fifth House and the sign Leo are ruled by the sun (each sign has a planetary ruler, and in this sense the sun is considered a planet), this is especially powerful for me.

In *Astrology, Psychology, and the Four Elements*, Mr. Arroyo talks about the Fifth House:

> These people want to be significant in some way. A person with a strong creative bent (Fifth House) finds that he has to produce something in order to feel good about himself. A strong emphasis on the Fifth House in the natal chart indicates that the individual must project himself into the world, that he must exercise his creative powers responsibly and consistently in order to attain the sense of joy and security he needs.

When I read this I knew I had to delve further into astrology, for this description fit me to a T. I had the intense need to creatively express myself through writing, songwriting, singing, and acting. When I thought about where I was now in relation to music, the phrase "he must exercise his creative powers responsibly," was not lost on me.

In his expansive *Astrology, Karma and Transformation*, Mr. Arroyo had more to say on the Fifth House.

> The Fifth House and its planets reveal creative resources which can be tapped in abundance....Since the Fifth House corresponds to the Sun's own sign, Leo, it is not surprising that I have gradually become inclined to consider this house as the strongest house in the chart after the First; for the Fifth House emphasizes not only the individual's creative potentials but also vibrations that characterize overt ways of pouring forth his or her energies spontaneously....

This pouring forth of one's energies also was characteristic of my sun sign Aquarius, the water bearer, also in the Fifth House.

> ...the Fifth House shows either the power of love or the love of power. At best it indicates one's capacity for letting

God's love and light flow through you and a simple trust in the goodness of life itself. It is related to our ability to allow the creative forces of life to manifest through us, as shown by its connections with children of both mind and body (the desire to have something greater than our limited ego be born through us). Both children and true creativity teach us the lesson that we must do what we love to do in order to attain a joyous sense of vitality.

In looking at what other planets occupied my Fifth House I found more clues. I learned that Mercury and the North Node of the Moon accompanied my sun in Aquarius in the Fifth House--and they all conjuncted one another. Terrific! What did it mean?

Quoting again on Mercury from Ms. Green's *Relating*, she states, "He is primarily the symbol of the urge to understand, to integrate unconscious motives with conscious recognition...." The urge that Mercury represented, according to Mr. Arroyo, was to express one's perceptions and intelligence through skill or speech.

Ms. Greene concludes, "Mercury is the sun's messenger, and while the sun is the symbol of the essence, Mercury is the symbol of that function which enables us to know the essence."

This really intrigued me, considering that my sun was conjunct Mercury--the sun's messenger, and all in the Fifth House, which again is ruled by the sun.

"Any conjunction between two planets in an individual chart," Mr. Arroyo states, "should be regarded as important since it indicates an intense merging and interaction of two life energies" (symbolized by the planets). The conjunction is the most powerful aspect in astrology. The most important and powerful of all conjunctions are those involving one of the "personal planets" (Sun, Moon, Mercury, Venus, and Mars) or the Ascendant. (As I've mentioned, I had the sun conjunct Mercury.) Such conjunctions almost always characterize dominant dimensions of the person's life, overriding motives and needs, and particularly strong modes of energy flow and personal expression.

Based on what I had gotten so far, I was to learn something (symbolized by Mercury), and after I became conscious of group life (Aquarius) I then creatively would express (through the Fifth House) this knowledge to share in the growth of the collective unconscious.

Maybe having Mercury (the desire to know) conjunct (intensely merged) with my sun (the urge for self-realization) was what was behind my existential quest. Maybe that was why I had no need for the status quo and needed to go beyond the surface of things. With all of these energies burning in the house of creativity (the Fifth House), maybe that was why I needed to love what I was doing--to be creative, to be free in self-expression--or to pay the harsh price of spiritual suffocation as I did many times when my economical states forced me to compromise.

Since Mercury had to do with communication primarily through writing or speech, it wasn't so surprising to me that it resided in the creative Fifth House, or that writing was something that I was compelled to do and came to me naturally.

I did wonder, though, about one thing. If Mercury was the symbol of the function that enabled one to know the essence, and the sun was the essence, and they were intensely merged by the conjunction aspect, then why didn't I come into this life with this knowledge that I was supposed to pass onto others? Why was I still in search of it?

It seemed to me that this conjunction of my sun with Mercury, this marriage of energies that took place as I slid down the birth canal, would have produced an offspring in consciousness, a knowingness inside of me. Maybe it had and I had not yet discovered it. Maybe, too, this powerful conjunction was responsible for the deep yearnings that propelled me on my quest to know. Finally, maybe through creativity, as I always had suspected, I would find release, fulfillment, and the answers to the questions that haunted my soul.

Since the north node of the Moon, as I've mentioned, also was contained in my Fifth House in Aquarius along with my sun and Mercury (and conjuncting them both), this was the next aspect of my chart I investigated.

I never had even heard of such a thing as a Moon node, much less dreamed it would appear in one's birth chart or could mean much of anything. But coupling what I was to learn from Martin Schulman's illuminating *Karmic Astrology: The Moon's Nodes and Reincarnation*, volume 1 with what I already had discovered about my chart, my thinking was to change.

To quote Mr. Schulman, "Many astrologers believe that the nodes hold more importance than the rest of the chart."

I found this to be very obscure. But then as I researched astrology more I found there were at least two camps out there: the mundane astrologers who viewed the different symbolisms involved quite superficially, almost stereotypically; and the esoteric, karmic, or spiritual astrologers, who in cases like Liz Greene married astrology to Jungian psychology.

Mr. Schulman was obviously of the later variety. He writes

> It is through the nodes that Western astrology is now able to make its first inroads into relating this divine science to the Hindu concept of reincarnation.
>
> The nodes represent the cause and effect relationships by which you lead your life. They are the difference between mundane and spiritual astrology....The nodes place the individual on his stairway to heaven insofar as they define the karmic lessons he has chosen to take on in this life....The soul continually expands its consciousness through its scope of experience until it is no longer necessary for it to reincarnate into a physical body....
>
> Man is constantly seeking his way home...and his karmic lessons are his road map complete with stop signs, obstacles and detours that he must overcome in order to bring his soul to the state of perfection where it can again become one with Pure Spirit.

I learned that the nodes had a north and a south end. "The north node is the symbol of the future....It symbolizes the highest area of expression to be reached in the current life and therefore must be interpreted by the highest qualities of the sign and house in which it is placed...."

Mr. Schulman calls the south node one's Achilles heel, and, "The potentially weakest spot in any horoscope...for it represents the footsteps we have left behind us....In fact an individual's most negative traits are those which for hundreds or thousands of years he has allowed to continue brewing within his soul."

Mr. Schulman concludes

> ...man does not achieve his north node until after he rises to the highest karmic levels of his south node. He must learn to give up gracefully the negative habits and memories which no longer serve a useful purpose in his life....
>
> The most amazing feature about the north node is that however much man achieves it, there is always more to go--as it truly represents his everlasting upward spiral towards God.

Now I needed to see how all this related to my chart and if I would buy into it.

According to Mr. Schulman

The Leo south node symbolizes prior lives where much revolved around the self. The north node in Aquarius points to the future of service for mankind, where the individual will assume the role of the "Waterbearer," so that he may be an instrument in the crusade for world evolution. Before he can do this, the enormous power of the Leo south node must be dealt with....

His karma now is to learn to walk lightly, without leaving footsteps....He must learn how to shed masks, ultimately discovering that ego-centered displays of dignity are coming from past-life habits....

Through his Aquarius north node he learns to overcome his past-life sense of prestige and develops the concept of Universal Brotherhood. He must ultimately come to see himself as part of a larger cosmic sphere, in which his role is to share in the burden of human evolution. He will reach his greatest happiness when he is able to set aside his own needs and substitute in their place a new humanitarian attitude toward all he sees around him....

Through his north node he is given the promise of a unique adventure, through which he can make an important contribution to the progress of civilization.

This information answered a lot of questions for me. I kept wondering why, after coming into spirituality as intensely as I had, I had put music so far into the background. I had been writing songs for so many years, and now it seemed to me that I was treating spirituality as if it were an end in itself.

As I've mentioned earlier, there was a fair amount of ego involved in wanting to be a successful musician. However, I did also have the strong, almost overwhelming desire to earn my living in creative ways. To do otherwise I likened to "buying existence," which for me was the kiss of death.

With the growing I had done, I saw in retrospective that my initial reasons for wanting to be an actor and for performing the songs I had written really were calls for love. But since I was developing a much stronger sense of self-love, I now had different reasons for pursuing my art. I was beginning to have more of a sense of responsibility about it, too.

I started to think again about writing the book that the two tarot card readers said they saw in my future. I had begun the book, but quickly abandoned it. Ego, in the sense of "Who am I to write this book?", kept popping up and preventing me from proceeding with it.

But with this information on the karmic nodes, I thought perhaps I would be able to serve humanity by writing about my spiritual experiences. At the same time I would be doing something creative--writing--while balancing karma.

Since I was able to relate to the information I read on the signs my nodes occupied, I next looked at what Mr. Schulman had to say about the house placements of my nodes.

> His karma is to learn the importance of dreams, inasmuch as how they explain his life. Ultimately he comes to realize that his entire existence has consisted of acting out his dreams, to the point that he has become the puppet of his own fantasies....
>
> He must realize that through his Fifth House north node he is now given the greatest gift that man can receive--the power to create his own destiny. By studying the process of creation, he can become aware that it is his own thoughts that have caused all the circumstances that he deems real in his life. He must then go further to understand the link between his thought and his dreams, for truly it is his life of dreams that in greater measure than he thinks is creating his life on earth.
>
> He must learn to be responsible about his dreams and careful of what he wishes for since he, more than one with any other nodal position in the zodiac, will actually see his dreams materialize....
>
> He is learning that the dreams of his Eleventh House south node are under the rulership of Aquarius, where they must be dedicated towards a service for humanity, and that the more he wishes for others the more he will ultimately have for himself....
>
> Some highly evolved souls with these nodes have experienced Cosmic Consciousness in a former life. Now through their Fifth House north node they are here to bring this awareness to the children of earth.

This certainly gave me a lot to think about. But I wasn't about to consider entertaining the possibility that I had achieved Cosmic Consciousness in a previous life. I had enough ego stuff to work on.

However, through my spiritual adventure I had to admit that I did learn quite a bit about manifesting. I also had some positive experiences experimenting with things like affirmations and lucid dreaming as ways of bringing into fruition that which I desired. So maybe sharing what I had learned in a book would be something I was destined to do. It was an overwhelming load to consider, even without the many personal issues stopping me. But for the moment I put it on back burner along with music.

Another area in my chart that I would like to share deals with Pluto. Pluto is the planet symbolic of death and rebirth, transformation, the occult, and sex--an experience also inclusive of the death and rebirth themes. Since my discussion here to a large extent has to do with karma and the value of astrology in this regard, I thought it fitting to include this material.

According to Mr. Arroyo, Pluto's urge represents "total rebirth; [the] urge to penetrate to the core of experience."

Its need was "...to refine [the] self, [the] need to let go of the old through pain." Of course we see this recurring theme of new life being born out of what has died throughout the earth plane, with one of the most obvious examples being the change of seasons.

After reading passages like these, I knew that Pluto was worth looking at more closely. It was clear to me that this new knowledge of Pluto's role in my chart would clarify or further reinforce the information I received on my north and south nodes of the Moon.

Quoting from Jeff Green's remarkable *Pluto: The Evolutionary Journey of the Soul*, volume 1, Mr. Green writes

> Individuals who have Pluto in...Leo [as in my chart] have been learning the evolutionary lesson of creative self-actualization....As such these people will feel as though they have a special destiny to fulfill....As a result, these individuals will deeply sense this special purpose in the depths of their Souls....The individual must learn to link their special destiny and creative purpose to a socially useful or relevant function....By learning the necessary lessons of objectivity and detachment, [these] individuals can also realize that they are not the source of creativity; they are a channel for the expression of the creative principle in the universe....

Once these evolutionary lessons are put in motion with conscious intent, these individuals can create something new and unique in whatever field of endeavor they are destined to fulfill. That which they create can have uncommon depth and power of a transformative nature.

This passage made me think again of my "spirit broadcast" alerting me to not feel special for whatever it was I would be doing. I found more clarification in this regard when I read what Mr. Green had to say about Pluto in the Eleventh House, the house Pluto occupies on my chart. I paid extra attention to what I was about to read, for the Eleventh House was Aquarius's natural house (and as I've already mentioned, my sun was in Aquarius).

These individuals have a natural innovative capacity because of their need to explore new approaches that allow for ongoing personal discovery....These are the individuals who have and will be classified by society as bizarre, radical, revolutionary, [all Uranian traits; Uranus rules Aquarius and the Eleventh House], or just "different."

This was no news to me because I had felt different from most people I met all my life. Maybe that was another clarification point for me. It wasn't so much that I felt special, but more that I *knew* I was different. Yet I did feel that I had some special destiny to fulfill.

Mr. Green continues

The evolutionary necessity to learn lessons of objectivity, detachment, and the need to sever all attachments that prevent growth can occur through the experience of intense emotional, intellectual, spiritual, or physical shocks....

The eleventh house...archetypes are very important for all of us because they offer the opportunity to revolutionize ourselves....It allows us to experiment with new thoughts or desires that radically transform who we have been and who we are now....

By learning these lessons, Eleventh House Pluto individuals can play a variety of socially meaningful roles. Their natural inventiveness and creativity can shine. The resulting metamorphosis will produce self-confident individuals who possess the power to understand objectively who they are, what they are, why they are the way that they are, and how best to actualize their own creative purpose within the context of a social need. In this understanding these individuals can assume socially relevant and meaningful roles, roles that have the power and potential to transform the existing barriers that are restricting future growth and evolution in the area of life to which they have applied themselves. In the same way, these individuals can promote this understanding in other people, even in whole nations.

One of the last things that I noticed in my chart had to do with the Eighth House. This was Scorpio's natural house, and its ruler was Pluto. In this house I found Jupiter in the sign of Taurus.

Jupiter's urge was to connect the self with something greater than the self, and it was the planet that expanded whatever it came in contact with.

The sign Taurus had to do with the appreciation of physical sensations; it was symbolic of the Earth mother. A planet found in this sign could be shaded by possessiveness and steadiness, according to Mr. Arroyo.

A mundane reading of this information could be an expansiveness (Jupiter) in a field of experience (the house) such as the occult ("that which is hidden," a typical Scorpionic theme), sex, or transformation--all concerns of the Eighth House.

Relating this information with what I already had discovered, I then realized that the mundane reading--the expansion of the occult and transformation (an expansion in and of itself) themes--applied in my case.

I totally was absorbed by metaphysics and with my own transformation. I proceeded with a certain steadiness, or so I felt, which was indicative of Taurus occupying the Eighth House.

This reading of my chart, coupled with my sun conjunct Mercury and the north node of the Moon in the Fifth House--all in Aquarius, led me to believe that I could communicate (Mercury) my experience with rebirth themes, and the occult (the expanded [Jupiter] Eighth House) to the world (Aquarius). With Pluto (the ruler of Scorpio and the Eighth House) in my Eleventh House (Aquarius's natural house), it seemed like some kind of interaction with group (Aquarius) transformation (Pluto) was in the cards for me.

Maybe I would write that book.

As I've stated earlier, one was not necessarily one's sun sign or prey to any other aspect found in one's chart. One's chart was simply a blueprint that could be read in a number of different ways. It indeed was possible to transcend many negative characteristics and to integrate the positive attributes found in the different planetary aspects in one's chart.

Finally, the information received through astrology or any other form of divination such as the I Ching, Tarot, or trance channeling, needs to be evaluated by the recipient through their own intuition.

As Brugh Joy points out in *Joy's Way*,

> There is a very real danger of displacing the power of direct consciousness awareness on to any of these objects or vehicles, in which case they can actually interfere with the opening of the direct channel. Initially, dreams, the Tarot, and the I Ching are to make one more self-aware. As with any good teacher, they fall away as one enters more deeply into the states of direct knowledge.

Chapter 25

Plateaus, Volcanoes, and Regeneration

I didn't know what it was, but after a year of metaphysical and spiritual classes, experiences, and constant reading, I started feeling like I was being too hard on myself.

Disciplining myself by quitting coffee, sugar, red meat, and hard alcohol had been a big sacrifice for me. Since obtaining proof that reincarnation was a fact, I scrutinized my every move so as not to accrue more karma. Taking Jesus' "Do unto others..." to the utmost extreme, I consistently looked at things from the other person's point of view. I did this so much that I think I was slowly driving myself crazy. I was becoming too self-conscious.

While I was glad to be making good money, which enabled me to take the classes and buy the books that helped move me further along in my spiritual search, the job's novelty had worn off months before and I was burning out.

I also was feeling like I was on a plateau and the magic that had accompanied my ascent into spirituality had lost its luster. I was getting bored.

So I finally gave up and decided to move back into the "real world" again. In my protest I cut back on reading spiritual material. I began watching television. I also felt a little guilty for my changed behavior. But the rebellious side of me overshadowed the guilt.

I don't know that I could say that I was happier this way, but I noticed that it did take the edge off how I had been feeling. At worst, it was a nice respite.

At the same time a friend had a room available in his two- bed-room apartment. While I had a history of roommate problems in the past, I reasoned that living with just one other person--and one who I was at least friends with--would be less of a strain than the compromise of living with a houseful of strangers. It actually might be fun for a while.

Things went fairly smoothly for the first few months, and as to be expected, as time went on little things began popping up. We had a few blowouts, but we basically were reasonable people who resolved our differences quickly.

But nonetheless, I was aware that in spite of my plateau rebellion period, I really had changed. No matter how much I tried stuffing down what I had become, it always was there. Like Lot's wife, there was no turning back without consequences. While I consciously had placed myself in this new environment, I unconsciously began projecting what I disliked about it and myself onto my friend.

In our sixth month as roommates together, we had synchronous stresses in our lives. Tom had all the financial headaches and frustrations associated with purchasing a new piece of property. I had dissatisfactions both with work and within myself creating friction.

At this time we stumbled upon a package deal to Hawaii so ridiculously inexpensive that we immediately made reservations, hoping that the rest and relaxation would assuage our collective tensions. I suppose I just as easily could have meditated, but hopping a plane to vacationland seemed more the ticket to me at the time.

Unfortunately (or fortunately) for me, the trip only served to magnify our glaring differences and how much I had changed. And I didn't know where I wanted to be anymore. It was one of the first vacations I had taken where I couldn't wait for the trip to be over. I was experiencing high anxiety made worse by the muggy tropical weather.

One of the only things that placated me was a book on Buddha that I found in the spot that the Bible usually occupies in hotel rooms. I took it with me wherever I went. In retrospect I'm sure I resembled Franny from J.D. Salinger's *Franny and Zooey*, with her *The Way of a Pilgrim* book. Even so, my life-imitating-art act wasn't so comfortable.

I even squeezed in the token vacation fling at the last minute to pretend that I was having a good time. While it was pleasurable, it had the same effect on me as a tranquilizer. It gave temporary relief. Then I was on another plane--an airplane, that is.

The minute I arrived home from Hawaii, the phone rang. I raced to my room, dumped my bag, and grabbed the receiver. It was my friend Santi, just back from Australia, calling to invite me to a workshop that he and a woman named Jill Jarrett would begin facilitating later that day.

"Is it free?" I asked sardonically.

"Oh, good golly no!" Santi cheerfully replied. He had such an endearing way about him. Even receiving bad news never seemed quite so bad coming from Santi.

"I just walked in the door from Hawaii and I'm broke," I reported.

"If you want to come we can work something out."

"I just got back from vacation, and now I feel like I really need a vacation!"

I really was low on cash, but even with my head still whirling in confusion I knew I needed to be at this workshop. Maybe something would surface there.

"I know it's not much, but I've got about 25 bucks I could put down," I finally said with commitment.

"All right!" he cheered, like I had just won the triathlon.

I knew he sincerely was happy that I would be joining the group, and I always could sense when Santi had something new and enriching to offer from his bag of spiritual tricks and treats.

He gave me directions to the retreat site where the weekend workshop would take place. I thanked him for the call, and we enthusiastically said our temporary good-byes.

I quickly emptied my suitcase out onto the center of my bedroom floor and rummaged through for some salvageable clean clothes for the weekend.

Newly packed, I headed for the stairs, and yelled over to Tom, still unpacking in his room on the other side of the condo, that I would be gone for the weekend. And I was out the door.

In the course of our brief conversation, Santi had explained that the workshop would incorporate exercises for mind, body, and spirit with a special emphasis on the latter two. We also would do a group rebirthing session at one point during the workshop. I had vaguely remembered hearing about rebirthing years earlier, at a time when I had not yet embarked on the spiritual path. But I never did get a clear understanding as to what it was all about. Here was an opportunity to experience it firsthand. With the exuberance in Santi's voice when he spoke about it, I knew it would be a remarkable experience.

When I drove onto the rambling, magnificent grounds, complete with boulders, wild flowers, and graceful trees, I knew I was home. The retreat center had been a convent in its most recent past life, so maybe that accounted for the peace and tranquility I felt waft in through my car as I toured the estate. There was a sadness there as well. Someone or something had died there.

Angels! That was it! The atmosphere was charged with angelic energy that no doubt comforted those in need here, as in Wim Wenders' poignant and masterful film *Wings of Desire*. But what did I desire? peace of mind? clarity? direction? all of the above? Yes!

The workshop was very small. In fact, I think there were only three or four of us in attendance. We did many body-oriented things. We jumped around. We learned graceful, meditative Tai Chi Chan. Then there was a body-and-breath-coordinated exercise called the Bow and Curl that Jill had devised as a way of proving that in an otherwise uncomfortable body situation one still could breathe and feel safe.

Since we were doing a lot of emotional work, I supposed these exercises served as a balance with which to get back into our bodies and ground ourselves.

We opened ourselves up--sometimes reluctantly. We shared what was going on in our lives. We talked about what we wanted in our lives and what was missing.

We meditated each day. We worked on dreams, which in many instances mirrored back what was being worked on or being worked out through the workshop.

We did a group rebirthing.

For this experience we each laid on the floor with a blanket. We then were coached to breathe in a certain rhythmic fashion. It was a circular breath whereby the inhale and exhale were identical. Santi and Jill, both of whom had completed the rebirthing training, crawled around on the floor to attend to us.

I don't quite remember how long it took, but I then heard the others begin crying on the floor next to me. Then I, too, began to cry. But it wasn't a painful crying--at least for me, for they were tears of joy. It felt wonderful!

All of us were crying like babies in the newborn ward. It was cozy, safe, and comfortable. Then I started laughing. It was so strange, but it felt really good. It was a much-needed release.

When I got back to my room that night, I had reached some conclusions. I wanted to continue rebirthing. I felt as though I was getting my life back. I wanted to be around like-minded people now, people who wanted to work on themselves and be healed. I also flirted with the idea of becoming a healer of some sort.

When I returned from the workshop and informed Tom of my

plans to move into my own place again, he was slightly flabber-gasted. He finally had purchased the piece of property, and we had just moved in when I gave notice. I tried explaining that it had noth-ing to do with the place or with him, but I needed to be in my own space.

Tom wasn't the only one who was surprised by my behavior. The next day at work I got some interesting reactions. Obviously, when we relate to one another we're each part of a chemical reaction. When one of the chemicals is altered, so is the exchange. This didn't bother me much, however. For many of these people were not exactly open to the idea of a spiritual search in the first place--much less the idea of working on themselves. So I tried my best to ignore them. This was one of the challenges I learned that accompanied raising one's vibra-tion in consciousness.

That night I called Santi and told him about what a wonderful day I had, and I thanked him again for the workshop. I then shared with him my desire to complete the rebirthing process when I could afford it. This usually was a ten-session commitment. He was very happy about my decision, and then he got very quiet.

"Steve," he humbly began, " I would be in more pain knowing that you're ready to do the rebirthing and unable to do so because of finances than being put out for having to wait for you to pay me."

"Could you please repeat that?" I asked, a little confused.

"What I'm saying is, if you're ready to do the rebirthing now, I would be in favor of you doing so and paying me when you can afford to."

I already had run up a bill for the workshop, and now he was willing to extend my credit?

My life was truly blessed. I couldn't believe it. Not only was the adage "When the student is ready, the teacher is there" beginning to be truer and truer for me, but the workshop and the rebirthing came to me at a time when I was lost and most in need of direction.

Santi recommend I read Leonard Orr and Sondra Ray's *Rebirthing in the New Age*, the first book written on the subject, before I began my first formal one-on-one rebirthing session. I gladly jotted down the title. Since I had taken a sabbatical from spiritually oriented read-ing material, I couldn't wait to get my hands on this book. Since I had a good experience with rebirthing over the weekend, I especially was ready.

Chapter 26

"Love as Much as You Can From Wherever You Are"

--Thaddeus Golas

I learned through the Orr and Ray rebirthing book that rebirthing was a way of getting rid of the negative energy patterns that were stored in the cells of the body and prevented us from being all we are--which is perfection.

These negative patterns or factors that cause unhappiness and can distort our view of ourselves and the world are dubbed the "Five Biggies." They include the birth trauma, the parental disapproval syndrome (PDS), specific negatives, the unconscious death urge, and other lifetimes.

Not only is being born a traumatic experience, but since we had amniotic fluid in our lungs prior to being born, we experienced the sensation of death by drowning as we struggled to take our first breaths. One of the conclusions that we came to was that it is not safe to breathe; another is that being out of the womb is unpleasant. Consequently, it is estimated that 90 percent of our fears originated at the time of our births.

According to Orr and Ray:

> The purpose of rebirthing is to remember, and re-experience one's birth; to relive physiologically, psychologically, and spiritually the moment of one's first breath--and release the trauma of it.

> In addition to healing the damage done by the birth trauma to the individual consciousness, it has been found that rebirthing repairs the damage done to the breathing mechanism at birth and removes blocks where the inner and outer breath meet, so that Infinite Energy and Infinite Being always

becomes easily available to the human body. Ultimately we may learn that rebirthing is a physical experience of Infinite Being which is not exclusively to do with the birth trauma. We do know from experience that rebirthing merges the inner and outer breath, which creates a bridge between the physical and the spiritual dimensions. This connection unites the human body to the prenatal life energy that built it originally, and thereby rejuvenates the body and frees the individual consciousness, not just from the birth trauma, but any kind of trauma.

The breathing method, as I've already briefly explained, was a rhythmic circular breath, whereby large quantities of air were pulled in and exhaled (usually through the mouth). This method brings more air into the body than breathing through the nose.

Quoting again from *Rebirthing in the New Age*:

At some point in rebirthing there is a re-connection to Divine Energy and as a result you may experience vibrating and tingling in your body....

If there is resistance of fear, then the body will tingle and vibrate. The vibration is not the energy but resistance to the energy...the tingling and vibrating is "God loving you at a cellular level"....At the completion of a rebirthing cycle resistance is dissolved and the person is breathing faster and there is no tingling.

Ten sessions with a trained rebirther were recommended, after which time, having processed a large chunk of their "stuff" and being more comfortable with the breathing process, one could rebirth themselves.

The Orr and Ray book contained a number of case studies that I found both informative and fascinating. But since rebirthing is a subjective experience, nothing could have prepared me for what I experienced in my first session or the sessions that followed.

The winding country roads I traveled to get to Santi's house were right out of *The Legend of Sleepy Hollow*. One of these roads was named Tunnel Road. This bit of synchronicity was not lost on me, as I was on my way to my first official rebirthing session--which might very well include a trip down one such tunnel or canal.

I was very excited about being able to go through the rebirthing process based upon my experience with it over the weekend workshop. I was open. I was enthusiastic. Having read *Rebirthing in the New Age,* I felt prepared for whatever might happen to me. Of course, I would have my good and loving friend Santi at my side coaching me through the experience.

Santi met me at the door with his usual big hug. We then settled into the tiny room and chatted about what was going on in my life. We probably conversed for about 45 minutes. Then Santi led me to some blankets and a pillow on the floor. I got comfortable while Santi said a short prayer asking for my guides, teachers, and master teachers to be present for the session.

Santi then mimicked a certain way of breathing that he wanted me to duplicate. He breathed rapidly through his mouth, similar to the way people breathe when they're trying to catch their breaths. This seemed a little different to me than how I had remembered it from the workshop, but I trusted both Santi and the rebirthing process. So with the blanket pulled up to my chin, I began breathing in this exaggerated fashion.

I was instructed to talk only when necessary and only when exhaling. But being a writer, I was compelled to report my up-to-the-moment impressions and feelings.

It wasn't long before I felt an odd tingling in my hands, which I reported to Santi. This was something new. I hadn't experienced this in the group rebirthing.

"Good!" Santi exclaimed.

Tingling was an understatement, it was such an intense vibration that I thought I could hear it buzz. My hands were starting to feel like baseball cards in the spokes of the wheel of a bicycle whirling at top speeds.

After an hour and a half of breathing, this vibrating had not only intensified, but it also spread to my entire body. My hands by now were contorting of their own accord into a fetal pose. They were buzzing on the inside like electric vibrators and cramping in what best can be described as awkward pain.

I felt like I had been hooked up to a jacuzzi through an intravenous tube! I was pinned to the floor. I couldn't have moved even if I had wanted to. I felt like I was about to blast off as I stared at the ceiling.

The monotony of my breathing and the intense vibrations fiercely shaking throughout my body took me to my limit. I panicked.

"Let me out of here!" I screamed. The suddenness of hearing my own voice shocked me. For the next few moments--I have no idea how long it was--I blanked out. What brought me back into consciousness was a single word.

"Breathe!" Santi screamed in my face.

Apparently in my shock I had stopped breathing, but only for a few seconds. Now conscious and breathing as he continued to coach me, I saw a saint in my mind's eye. It was either St. Anthony or St. Jude, I wasn't exactly up on my saints. He had a staff that he was holding at a 45-degree angle to the ground. This vision reassured me. Then I got a flash of some caverns. Was this a memory of the birth canal?

As I continued to breathe, I noticed that the vibrating had changed, the cramping had stopped, and it now actually was quite pleasant. My entire body felt orgasmic. The energy cascaded over me repeatedly. I felt calm, blissful, at peace. I felt so close to God, like my body had returned to its ethereal substance and I was one with all.

When this altered state faded and I began breathing normally, Santi handed me a cupful of purified water. Apparently it was important to drink lots of water while going through the rebirthing process.

Eventually I got up--and that was an experience in itself. Santi and I talked about what had happened. He reminded me that the tetany I had experienced, the intense vibrations, were caused by my fear and resistance. As I had remembered from the rebirthing book, fast breathing lessened the painful cramping. In some extreme cases temporary paralysis actually occurred.

In my case, when I was coached to breathe faster after the tetany began, the vibrations came on like gangbusters, which frightened me to the point where I screamed out. If I had been somehow better prepared for this ingeniously novel experience, or at least knew for how long I could expect these powerful vibrations to continue, maybe I could have gone the distance.

When I later went back to the rebirthing books I had read, I learned that there was a distinction to be made between the intense vibrations and the tetany. Orr and Ray stated that the "...vibration is the cleansing process and should be welcomed...rapid breathing is dissolving and pumping out tension and negative thought from the body and vibrating is incidental to the cleansing process."

According to *Rebirthing: The Science of Enjoying All Your Life* by Jim Leonard and Phil Lout, tetany was

> ...the involuntary tightening of muscles during rebirthing. It occurs most commonly in the hands....Tetany is caused by controlling the out breath....People go into tetany

when they have "control patterns"....If a pattern is coming up that the unconscious mind deems too threatening to the conscious mind's self-delusion, then the person may control the exhale in order to hide. This results in tetany, which itself can serve as a marvelous smokescreen for hiding from what one fears....

I wasn't sure what I was hiding or fearing since it mainly was subconscious. Maybe, at the least, I was afraid of the unknown. But I did know one thing. While this rebirthing business had scared me half to death, like William Hurt's character in *Altered States* after he submerged from the deprivation tank, I knew I was onto something major. It was after having an inkling as to what I was getting into that I made a commitment to myself that no matter how difficult it got, I would complete the ten recommended rebirthing sessions.

It was absolutely amazing to me! I had gone into an altered state, had been overwhelmed physically, and had contact with the angelic realm, simply through the use of "the breath" (as Santi frequently would refer to it). I was stupefied to think that I could have undergone such dramatic experiences by simply breathing!

For a long time I had wanted to glimpse other dimensions and gain self-clarity without the use of drugs. Drugs had been used for centuries in world religions, and journeying to one's core through drug use was how the drug culture began. I found it sad that not only were drugs abused, but many of those on drugs were oblivious to their intended use.

I always had believed that it was possible to reach other realities without the implementation of drugs, only I lacked the vehicle. Now with rebirthing, I was going on a trip--only I wasn't quite sure where.

That night I had some interesting dreams. In one dream someone was cutting into my side with a broken piece of glass. Over and over they'd slash me, yet there was no pain. As in the vestitures dream, there was no blood. My reaction to this intrusion was simply that I had had enough and that it was more of a nuisance than a painful experience.

I took the dream to symbolize that I was opening myself up, cutting through to get to my inner self. Like the tetany I had experienced, it was more of an awkward pain than really painful.

The second session, which occurred a week after the first, lasted only 45 minutes. The vibrations came fairly quickly this time, with that tyrant tetany following shortly thereafter.

I used the affirmation "God's love" on the inhale, and "relax" on the exhale. The use of these affirmations brought to mind a mosaic of the Virgin Mary and Jesus as a baby. They were painted with muted colors and tinged with gold.

Mary began speaking to me in the same voice as the woman in my direct spirit communique the previous Easter, only she was not broadcasting through the back of my head. Instead, the message was more telepathic.

She said, "Trust Santi, he's your friend."

I now changed my affirmation on the inhale to "life breath" and exhaled "release." These were not affirmations I found in books; instead I used what I felt would work for me. Out of necessity I always was improvising.

I still felt the buzzing vibrations and the intense cramping in my hands even when using the affirmations. I wished whatever I was holding in would come out, but all I could do was breathe and work with my affirmations.

The vibrations now also were buzzing in my jaw and around my head. I was starting to feel inhuman. It felt like I was transforming into the fly of movie fame!

Then I got a picture of the vibrating pressure circumnavigating my head, moving from under my chin, up the side, over the top, and back down the other side. My head seemed to be half inside and half outside of my mother's womb.

The combination of hands and head dually vibrating were especially intense. I breathed through it as best as I could. But the intensity dramatically increased and I didn't know how much more I could take. I didn't know how much more there *was* to take. I felt like I had gone through enough. So with pleading eyes, I told Santi I had to stop--I couldn't take anymore.

He told me there would come a time when he would no longer be able to do so. This made me feel "terrific" although I didn't know exactly what he meant, and I couldn't have cared less at that split second either, for I urgently needed to come down from this excruciating experience. He somehow guided my breathing in such a way that I came down from this intense trip.

At the beginning of the third session, I was a wreck. I began breathing in the circular fashion as before, but then stopped. I was terrified at the prospect of having to experience tetany again. Maybe I did fear losing control.

"Santi, I really don't feel like doing this today, I'm not in a very good emotional state."

At the time I said these words I meant them sincerely and was too wrapped up in my overwrought state to realize that if I had been all right emotionally I probably never would have opted to undergo the rebirthing process in the first place.

Laying on the floor with my blanket, I said, "I'm gonna go home."

"You know, Steve, I told you that on the fourth or fifth session many people never make it to their sessions. Their cars miraculously brake down. They suddenly have to fill in for someone at work. Something comes up."

"I know," I said, starting to get up, "but this is only my third session. So I'll come back next week to do this one."

My resistance was so high that it was as if I hadn't heard what he said. Santi then smiled at me so lovingly and compassionately that something got communicated at a deep level, and I somehow knew I wasn't going home just yet. All of a sudden I was overcome with emotion. I was confused and angry.

"Why do I have to do this?" I cried out. "Only two million people have gone through this out of 200 million. Why do I have to be in the guinea pig group? I'm not that screwed up anyway. I'll come back next week."

Then to my surprise I blurted out, "Why doesn't anyone love me?"

I began crying profusely. But not just crying. It was the same kind of involuntary action as throwing up. Just when you think you're done, you begin again. It didn't sound like me. I sounded and felt like a helpless little baby whose crying resounds without respite.

"Why am I crying?" I pleaded to Santi on the exhale.

"You weren't loved the way you needed to be loved."

"I know my family loves me. And my friends love me. But I just don't feel it!"

I must have cried for half an hour. Then I felt the pleasant orgasmic vibrations in my feet and hands and I had more visions.

Master Teacher Jesus was with me along with Saints Mary, Jude, and Anthony and a few friends who were going through rebirthing at the same time I was. I felt what I imagined to be the chakras opening up. It felt wonderful! I didn't want to move.

When the crying and the vibrations again faded and Santi and I had our post-session discussion, I finally understood my resistance to the session. Having to feel vulnerable to all my past hurt was something that I obviously had not wanted to face on a deep level.

One of the things I found most amazing with this last session was the release I experienced through tears. I was amazed I cried at all, but the utterly uncontrollable depth of emotion that accompanied the tears and my crying so unrelentingly really amazed me.

It was a slowly changing cliche that this society doesn't tolerate such emotions in men. But when I thought about it, outside of the weekend workshop and on a few other isolated occasions--like upon hearing that my grandmother, whom I was very close to, had had a second stroke and was not expected to live--did I ever release emotion through crying. The last time I cried was six years ago!

In re-reading parts of *Rebirthing: The Science of Enjoying All of Your Life*, I discovered a little section on suppression. In this book suppression was defined as "...diverting part of your energy to the purpose of holding back other parts of your energy, so you won't feel them." The section included a list of common chemical addictions and the things they suppressed. There was no judgment attached to this list, but it related that alcohol suppressed fear, nicotine suppressed anger and frustration, marijuana suppressed sadness, psychedelics suppress suppression, and caffeine and other stimulants such as cocaine served as artificial means of keeping the suppression going. It made sense that stimulants kept the suppression going since suppression was such an energy-draining activity.

After reading this section of the book, I remembered that I had been using marijuana recreationally for almost 15 years.

With the explanation that marijuana suppressed sadness, I not only could better understand its widespread use, especially while our country warred in Vietnam, but I also could understand why I had cried so profusely and uncontrollably during my rebirthing sessions.

I had stopped using marijuana for a year here or there, mostly as an experiment. But I enjoyed it so much, in addition to it stimulating my creativity (especially with music), I could see no reason to stop. Now I had a reason. In wanting to be as in touch with my feelings and in the moment as possible, I decided to give up the drug.

The fourth session was very powerful. Again I experienced the vibrations and tetany in my arms and hands. The same unrelenting sobbing accompanied these sensations. At one point I had an extremely profound knowingness that I had to absolutely love myself. It's hard for me to put into words the magnitude of these seemingly trite words. But I absolutely knew that I had to show people who I was and that I no longer could hide the feelings I had stuffed for so much of my life for fear of disapproval or punishment.

At this point, which was after the tears had cried themselves out, I began screaming and cursing everyone and every injustice I felt had been done to me. I jumped up to my feet and continued my tirade until I ravaged my vocal chords, rendering them useless.

A few days after this session, I began sharing parts of myself that I never had shared before with my parents, who were 3000 miles away. This was both frightening and illuminating. I cried through parts of these conversations, and felt that I finally was addressing my fear-of-intimacy issue with them. The fear is that sharing one's true feelings with others (especially loved ones) will result in rejection or some other form of abandonment.

In my case this sharing ultimately served to deepen my relationship with my parents and others. I guess I was one of the lucky ones. In conversations with friends in similar situations, there had been both those whose fear of intimacy was so intense that they couldn't muster the courage to confront it. Others either were ultimately rejected or not heard when they attempted to resolve these issues for themselves.

Although I previously hadn't mentioned it, it usually took a few days for me to integrate what had occurred in a rebirthing session. I was integrating both conscious and unconscious information, which yielded uncertainty or, at times, different levels of anxiety. For the most part I could handle it, but on one such occasion I was at my breaking point.

I was driving home from a day with friends on this particularly dark night. I only had a few exits on the freeway to go when a sweeping wave of anxiety came over me. In retrospect, I could see what this was, but at the time I thought I was about to jump out of my skin or go crazy!

Waves of heat surged through me. Since I experienced these uncertain feelings while driving, I especially was petrified. I gripped the wheel tightly in an attempt to hold onto it and myself at the same time.

I quickly pulled off the freeway at the next exit to sort out my feelings and attempt to ground myself. I parked in the lot of a liquor store and took some deep breaths. I was afraid to breathe in the rebirthing style for fear of bringing on tetany. Sitting in my car made me feel even more anxious, so I went into the store and bought some bottled water. I remembered that drinking water was important to the rebirthing process. But this didn't help, either. I felt that if I didn't come up with something soon, I would snap. I somehow forced myself to keep it together.

All I could think to do was call Santi. So out of complete desperation, I asked the young guy behind the counter if I could use the phone to make a local call, and that it was an emergency. Luckily, he complied.

The line rang once. Then twice. What if he wasn't home? I tightly gripped the phone and then the familiar, soothing voice of Santi came on the line.

While sitting on the floor so I would be inconspicuous, I explained what I was feeling to Santi. He tried his best to talk me down, but it wasn't working. My anxiety intensified.

"Santi, talk faster!" I demanded, not knowing how long I could hold on and not knowing what would happen if I did snap.

At this inauspicious moment the kid behind the counter told me I had to get off the phone because the owner was on his way to the store.

"I think there's a phone down the street. I'll call you right back," I breathlessly informed Santi.

I started running down the street--it would be faster than driving. I felt a chill. I didn't know if it was me or the weather. I brushed by the Montecito elite on their way to the restaurants and nightclubs that lined the road. To reassure myself, I asked someone if it was indeed a bit chilly. At least this was confirmed.

When I got to the deserted gas station on the corner, there was a phone as I had remembered. I quickly redialed Santi's number. When he answered, he asked me to recount all of the events of the day.

A police car was pulling into the station. My panic heightened. A male and female officer got out of the car. In my paranoia I told myself they were not coming for me. I forced myself to smile. They appeared to be walking toward me. They responded to my smile with nods, and walked in the other direction down the street. I breathed a sigh of relief from at least that situation.

I told Santi of my conversation with my parents in as much detail as I could remember. He then had a moment of "a-ha."

"It sounds like you're experiencing guilt."

"So what. Now what?" I responded, still uncertain as to how much more I could take before breaking.

He then coached me to breathe in a certain way. This helped a little. Next, he instructed me to couch the phone in the crook of my neck to free up my arms.

"Now raise your arms into the air and visualize white light coming out of the palms of your hands and being sent to your parents."

This seemed useless and hokey to me, but I was hardly in a position to argue.

Then using my parents' names, he gave me a little prayer to say as I continued spreading the white light in the direction of the East. I started to cry, and surprisingly I felt a little release. I continued this process for five minutes or so. Then Santi had me breathe again so he could hear the quality of it.

"Your breathing sounds all right to me. I think you'll be all right."

I did feel a little less anxious, and was reassured by his estimation of the cause of this anxiety attack.

"Now," he began, "do you think you can drive?"

"I'm not sure what will happen when I get back into the car, but I think I can. And I'm only an exit or two from my house."

"I think you'll make it all right, too. Now as soon as you get home, give me a call back."

"I will. Thanks, Santi."

I felt like I was on "Beat the Clock," the old television game show that had people doing bizarre stunts in specific time intervals. I raced back to my car and began my short journey.

I prayed out loud, taking in large quantities of the sea air. I actually was singing the "Our Father," gospel style. Only when I got to the word "evil" in "deliver us from evil," I started to panic again. So I sang only the first two lines of the prayer, over and over again until I reached home.

My roommate's dog greeted me at the door. I could feel her love. I felt a little better. I called Santi. We talked only briefly. I needed sleep. I was exhausted.

"Santi, thanks again. I love you."

"I love you, too, dear one. And remember, I'm always here."

I hung up the phone, fell back to my bed, and drifted into dreamland.

A few days later I went to a local deserted beach by myself. There were huge boulders blocking entrance to the sand and ocean. I didn't have the proper shoes on in which to traverse these obstacles, but I nonetheless felt drawn to the water that day for some reason.

On my way to the rocks, I encountered some mushy sand and a mudlike substance that also blocked my passage. Something obviously did not want me at the beach this day.

I stepped my sandal lightly into this muck to test it, only to feel myself sinking into it. My foot was entirely submerged in this junk. Now I had no choice, I had to get to the water!

With this slippery, gooey muck on my sandals, the rocks were really a challenge. My sandals flopped all over. At times I hesitated, but I made my way over the last of the giant rocks.

The velvety sand that I now touched was well worth the effort. When I reached the ocean to wash off my feet and sandals, my feet touched soft, smooth sand below the warm water instead of the jagged rocks that usually cut my feet. It felt absolutely wonderful!

When I was through washing and wading through the foamy tide, I headed back to the rocks. From this perspective point I noticed an easier climbing area, which I promptly took. But then I was back to the muck.

I spotted an area that was so dry that it cracked into a million mosaic tiles. I very gingerly tested this area with the tip of a toe to avoid sinking into this sludge again. But underneath this deceiving surface was more muck. Then from out of nowhere I found a little trail created by a series of flat rocks. Teetering and sliding, I crossed this makeshift bridge over troubled muck.

When I reached my car, I found 11 cents on the ground. I picked up the coins and took them as a symbol of some kind of mastery-- which the number 11 signifies. In fact, I saw the entire little impromptu adventure to symbolically mirror back what I had learned thus far through rebirthing. There were risks, obstacles, and all sorts of unexpected junk one needed to experience and explore in order to grow. But there also was absolute peace, tranquility, love, and beauty to be found in the process as well.

During the fifth session I was feeling the vibrations in my arms, hands, feet, and solar plexus. It felt pleasant, even though I again was crying. Even though it was not always necessary to consciously know what was being released, my mind at times needed to know.

Then the monotony of my breathing and the accompanying anxiety almost caused me to freak-out, as I had done in my first session. I experienced the fear of going crazy or being possessed. I began cursing and screaming out to whatever I imagined to be out there. In retrospect this little drama simply may have been symbolic of more resistance, an unconscious excuse to avoid dealing with another issue.

Santi was being as patient as ever with me, and after I finished my monologue of anger, he suggested I lay back down and resume breathing. Again I started to cry. This time I strongly felt the tears were a response to the fear of being born. After all, this was called rebirthing, although it was true that not everyone did in fact have the experience of reliving their births in rebirthing. I somehow sensed that I would.

I reasoned to myself that in re-experiencing my birth there more than likely would be more uncontrollable screaming. I feared doing severe damage to my already exhausted vocal chords in the process, so I somehow shut down.

At one point I saw a vision of a white dove in my mind's eye, where a dull pain ached in my head. I thought that my third eye was being worked on. I imagined that I shortly would be seeing a blinding white light and be reborn. But this did not happen.

I began my sixth session using the affirmation "God loves me" on the in-breath and "I love you, God" on the exhale. This helped to relax me. The vibrations were again in my hands, feet, and solar plexus. My mouth and the area around my head felt kind of numb, but it was more pleasurable than painful.

After an hour and a half of this, I started smiling, then laughing, and then breathing in and out quite rapidly. At this point Santi drew my legs up and gently pushed my knees to my chest. When he put his weight on my shins, I intuitively began to push.

"Push," he coached.

But it wasn't what I expected. It was effortless. Being born was easy. I felt wonderful.

The seventh session had me thinking that I was regressing. There was vibrating in my hands and head, and again I was crying profusely. When I asked for some kind of explanation, Santi gently reminded me that I did not receive the kind of love I needed.

By the eighth session I didn't know what to expect. I had been reborn in the sixth session, so why was I still doing this? I reasoned that I probably still had excess junk to clear out, so I continued to trust and proceed with the process.

I felt relaxed and mellow when I started breathing. Then I saw a kind of blue light on the ceiling. It was oval in shape. Then it turned to violet. Then there was a rainbow of colors in it--green, blue, and violet. Whatever this was had me transfixed.

"It's beautiful!" I said aloud. Then tears of joy rushed down my cheeks.

"Yes!" Santi nodded.

But how did he know what I was seeing?

Unexpectedly, I immediately went into processing. I wailed and found myself uncontrollably writhing back and forth on the floor.

The oval-shaped rainbow was gone. I had somehow become it. Something was taking hold of me, and I couldn't stop it. I was so intensely overwhelmed that I couldn't think. All I could do was hysterically breathe and sob and give into whatever was taking me over. I had to surrender.

There was no choice. No exit. It had begun.

Emersed in tears, I reached my arms out, desperately wanting to be held, to be rescued. Gasping for air, my breathing involuntarily increased. Now I was burning up. I was hyperventilating. There was no recourse. The heat intensified. Frantically, I ripped off all my clothes and rocked back and forth, sobbing in my primordial sweat. I have no conception of how long this lasted.

Then it stopped. I experienced a calm. I was in a profoundly altered state. It was a dreamlike dance in slow motion. I saw close-ups of nurses and doctors with face masks. They wore light blue shirts with white aprons. They were all lit up in a brightly glaring white light. I watched awestruck. I felt light as air. I had just been born.

When Santi and I had our post-session chat, it became clear to me that the session where he had pushed my knees to my chest was just a practice session to give me confidence that it's easy to be born.

My ninth session was divided into two parts out of necessity. I again was feeling the integrating anxiety, so I called Santi to have my session three or four days early.

As in most of my sessions, I wept. What I was consciously working on was being easier on myself. I breathed in the prescribed fashion, but even afterwards felt incomplete.

In the second part of the ninth session, I cried and got angry at the headache I had been having. I worked with the affirmation "I am peace, joy, love, and tranquility."

The most positive thing about the session was that I felt fairly certain that I could breathe by myself now. That is, I felt I could rebirth myself without supervision, which was one of the long-lasting, beneficial by-products of rebirthing. After one had completed the ten sessions, they could use "the breath" whenever necessary.

The tenth session was a form of graduation. I don't mean to imply that I was now "cured" and no longer needed to work on myself, but I did breathe in this session without coaching.

Again I had the feeling of not being loved. I cried and cried, and rocked myself to one side in the fetal position. As in all my sessions, when the crying had run it's course, I was left with unequaled peace and bliss.

I was finally at the place where I felt I was ready to breathe on my own. Even though I felt I was ready, there was some fear there as well. So when I finally laid down to breathe, I wasn't too surprised when tetany came on like gangbusters. At first I thought I wouldn't be able to handle it by myself, so I tried stopping the process by getting up and going to the kitchen for some water while breathing the whole time.

I realized that I was resisting, so I went without the water and returned to my bed and continued with the process. I spread my fingers apart to stop the cramping that the tetany caused in them. Continuing to breathe, it felt natural to roll on my side in the fetal position.

As I relaxed into the breathing, the painful aspect of tetany was replaced by the pleasurable vibrations. Both my hands and heart chakra were buzzing. I felt really good. Consequently, when I finished my first session alone, I proceeded on to have an especially wonderful day.

I now was able to employ this simple yet powerful tool whenever I needed it. It was truly a gift.

I continued rebirthing with Santi after the tenth session in addition to rebirthing on my own. I found that there were times while breathing alone that nothing seemed to happen and that it was helpful to have someone else's energy present while rebirthing. The extra bonus of rebirthing with Santi was that he was quite clairvoyant, and as I've mentioned, he conversed with his guides and teachers on a regular basis.

I remember one session with Santi whereby I breathed myself in the normal rebirthing fashion for the entire hour, and again nothing seemed to be happening. Toward the end of the hour, I mentioned this to Santi while I continued to breathe. He promptly went into trance and after a few minutes asked, "Do the colors orange and green mean anything to you?"

I immediately began to cry uncontrollably, for as I shared with Santi, those were the colors that I painted my bedroom when I was in high school in the late 1960s, a particularly unpleasant time in my life. This prompting on Santi's part brought more buried pain to the surface for release.

I don't know that I would have been able to release that on my own. In rebirthing oneself it's easy to fall asleep and space things out or to unconsciously resume normal breathing. These were all ways of resisting going into process, which may have accounted for my own seemingly nonproductive sessions. Yet while it is not always necessary to know what is being released, at this point in my evolution I liked having this information.

Chapter 27

The Healing Power
of Love

A few months after I was able to rebirth myself on my own, a major disappointment in a relationship sent me into a severe depression. While I had been depressed before at different times in my life, nothing compared to the state I now was in. I was a complete basket case, I felt like the living dead. I walked out of my job. I cried for weeks. I broke down in front of total strangers. I wasn't eating much. I had no reason to live. I had no life. I just didn't care.

Mornings were the worst. Santa Barbara was experiencing an Indian summer, and while I felt dark inside, golden light fought to pierce through my heavy, tightly drawn drapes. Only as the sun fell in the West each evening could I breathe in some relief. I could become invisible.

Had I not grown so much spiritually, I could have had an easier time of it. There was a liquor store a half block away, and I easily could have purchased harder drugs to numb the pain. But I knew now that I could not do that.

My behavior had alienated my "friends." In fact, apart from Santi, there were only one or two people I really could count on for support--although I wasn't exactly going out of my way to solicit help.

A few weeks into the depression I called my parents and shared with them what I was going through. I had not wanted to burden them with my pain. I knew that they loved me, as they always had supported me in one way or another, but at one point in the conversation I remember crying out, "but I just don't feel it!"

We love but we don't always express what we feel. Or perhaps our means of expression is inadequate and doesn't reach the people we hope to reach in the way they need to be reached. It was as Santi had stated over and over again, "You did not receive the love in the way you needed it."

He further pointed out that I was not alone in this regard--most people fit into this category as well. There was no one to blame for this lack. It simply existed.

Maybe, too, due to the depth of my depression I was too numb to feel anything, or maybe I had felt too cheated by love to trust, or too afraid to let myself feel love again because it always could be taken away.

The rebirthing had been a major step in opening me up, for in the course of the conversation with my parents something happened inside of me. I began to feel a shift. I could feel the depth of their love. I still was intensely depressed, but there now was another emotion operating inside of me. A little candle had been lit, and there now was some joy mixed in with the tears.

Santi was most supportive of me while I went through the depression. Even though I was capable of rebirthing myself, he gave me additional rebirthing sessions that I feel were stronger because of the his powerful healing energies.

I cried relentlessly in the sessions. Intense tears of grief mixed with whatever past stuff I needed to work out. In one session that stands out in my mind, I lay sobbing, and shortly after the vibrations began in my hands, there was a new sensation. It was hard to describe; it was like a slow hum. But I absolutely knew I was contacting a higher realm, for the feeling was that of transcendence. I could see myself literally bathing in a haze of white light. There was a supreme intelligence out there that came to those in need whose hearts were open. My heart now was open like an oozing wound, ravaged.

"It feels like there are hands lying on top of my hands," I whispered through my tear-streaked face to Santi.

"You're feeling God's hands," he replied with joy. Santi had seen so many different situations occur through his rebirthing training and in his practice, and was in contact with those in spirit on a regular basis, so I knew that this is fact what was happening.

I had had spiritual experiences that left me awestruck, but this connection that was now occurring was the most profound transfusion of pure love that I was yet to experience.

I lay in this state for maybe a half an hour. I was utterly mesmerized by the power and grace that were now flooding through me. I had been in so much pain, too weak to pick myself up, and now God/the universe was again by my side to revitalize me and reassure me that such a force indeed existed.

If there was no greater intelligence out there, then what was I feeling? Why did I "arbitrarily" have this life-altering experience now, when I was in such a state of despair and in need of so much love and healing?

One of the things I also did while going through the depression was meditate. I knew prayer was talking to God, and meditation was listening to Him, but now I used meditation mainly as escape.

I just had too much time on my hands. I only could sleep for so long, and I wasn't motivated to do much of anything else, so I meditated once or twice a day. I would attempt to contact Dr. Chang, who was one of my teachers in spirit. But I never knew how much was in my imagination and how much was information coming from this entity.

Most of my meditations weren't very memorable. In fact, for all I knew I may have fallen asleep. But I needed a respite from my extremely painful depressed state.

One morning in meditation, however, I did experience something that was new to me. I began this particular meditation by focusing on each body part, beginning with my feet and working my way up, relaxing each part in the process. This was another meditation technique that I learned from Santi.

There was a period of time that I have no recall of, the period between feeling relaxed and what occurred next. When I regained consciousness (or semi-consciousness), I was in some kind of funnel. It was dark yet it felt safe. There was a lot of what can best be described as tiny vertical strips of static electricity buzzing all around me. Somehow, I was being pulled up to a bright light. After a few minutes the scene began to pulsate to the degree that I could hear it. Then it further increased in its intensity.

I was now no longer just a participant in the experience, I was *becoming* the experience! I had become one with all of this disbursing energy, expanding and expanding. I didn't know what was behind this energy, the light or the dark, or what I was becoming, or where it was taking me.

My awareness level shifted to a lucid state, and I asked myself, *Where am I?*

I attempted to feel my body, but it was not there! I panicked and attempted reconnection with my body. I tried visualizing my room and the chair I had settled into when I began meditating. Then with a thud, I miraculously was back!

I quickly blinked my eyes open as I shook with the thumping beat of my heart. It was then that I remembered something that my friend, Dorothy, who I had met in one of Santi's spiritual development classes, had shared with me.

We were sitting in circle one evening, about to meditate, when Dorothy stole the group's attention.

"Wait! I have to tie this around someone's ankle," she pleaded, holding up a piece of string.

She explained that when she meditated, she frequently went out of her body, and she feared at times that she would not be able to return. So to keep her somewhat grounded, she tied a string around her ankle and then attached the other end to the ankle of the person sitting next to her when she meditated.

Most of us could not help laughing at this odd request. But since Dorothy was seated next to me, and since she was serious about this, I allowed her to attach the string to my ankle.

Now after this experience in the funnel, I realized that this was no laughing matter and maybe I, too, would need some form of ground before meditating.

Chapter 28

A Long Day's Journey
Back to Life

A few weeks before I became depressed, I decided that I would get back into acting again. A friend I met at work was involved with a local theatre group, and I planned to audition for it. A new production was in the works and auditions soon were to be held.

Since I had been so depressed, I had all but forgotten about this new venture of mine. So it took me a minute to collect my thoughts when I received a call informing me of the dates and times auditions would be held for some plays by Moliere that the local company planned to stage.

I jotted down this information and thanked the woman for calling. Since I had to audition for the theatre group, I would also have to prepare the customary monologue. The director suggested one of Edmond's speeches from O'Neill's *Long Day's Journey Into Night*. I never had read this play, although I was somewhat familiar with the story line.

There I was, emersed in my own despondent drama and reading another. I "loved" this aspect of life imitating art--as opposed to Woody Allen's axiom that art imitated life, and life imitated television. Reading this particular character's speech was beneficial to me in auditioning for the ensemble group in a strange and perverse way.

I usually found it difficult if not nearly impossible to employ the technique of "sense memory"--recalling a moment from one's life that would elicit a particular emotion and remember my lines at the same time. But now I could appreciate and employ the tool, and I didn't have to go too far back in memory to make it work for me, either.

After much thought I auditioned for the group. I really didn't feel like it, but something inside of me knew that I needed to get outside of myself, and this pushed me on. Acting was an all-encompassing experience in awareness, and I had been so completely listless that it would have to take something like this to crack me out of my shell.

I was accepted into the group and earned a few small parts in the upcoming Moliere shows. I have to admit that donning seventeenth-century garb each night and a long Pollyanna curled wig helped to get me out of myself.

At times, in costume, waiting in the green room for my cues, I would fall into the depression. But since I didn't look like me when I saw myself reflected back in the mirror, I got a little confused and wondered why I was feeling this way. It certainly had nothing in common with either role I played in the two one-act plays that we were performing.

The production ran for two or three months to good notices--even my little bits were noticed.

Chapter 29

Prophecies, Proof, and Intelligent Life in the Universe

When our theatrical run neared completion, I got hit with an astronomical rent increase. Santa Barbara was getting quite expensive, and without working I could no longer afford to live alone. So I again hit the streets in search of a new dwelling place.

I found a room in a house on the west side with about "a million" other people. All of them were spiritually minded in one way or another, but it still was tough living with five other people. The rent was cheap, which was my main consideration at that point, and I thought it would be good living with other people again.

During the first six months of that year I rebirthed myself each morning. I worked with my dreams, and I meditated. I still was somewhat depressed. But time went on, and it now was summer.

I was having a series of earthquake dreams. They were lucid in part, and my sense was that they were not symbolic dreams. But if they had been, the symbolism eluded me for the moment.

Santi was gone for a good part of the summer, along with Verna and some other people I had met through the institute. They were on a mountaintop just outside of Colorado Springs. It appeared that Verna had purchased some land there years earlier, intending to retire there one day. Information through spirit revealed that the land, which stood at a maximum elevation of 8,400 feet, matched the ley lines (invisible lines of energy) of Machu Pichu in Peru and the Great Pyramid of Giza in Egypt. The land was surrounded by a positively charged natural spiritual energy field.

For two summers now, the institute had been offering workshops on the mountain. The facilities included comfortable three-season tents, solar-heated water for showers, an open-air kitchen with a wood floor, a screened-in dining area, an event tent (left over from World War II) where classes were held, a sweat lodge, and a healing tepee.

As usual, Verna was facilitating a number of workshops on the mountain that summer. But the summer's highlight was Elwood Babbitt, the world renowned trance channel medium who resided in the Northeast and whose life and work had been documented in a number of books penned by Harvard professor and author Charles Hapgood.

I was hoping to travel to Colorado to attend some of the classes, but my finances and I still both were a little shaky. Yet I knew that I would at some point visit this mountain retreat, which later would formally be christened "The Blue Mountain Center."

At the end of August, when Santi returned from his stay at "Blue Mountain," he was filled with stories. In addition to the transformation and healing he had witnessed and experienced personally, he spoke of Elwood Babbitt. In fact, *everyone* was talking about Mr. Babbitt.

According to his biography, *Voices of Spirit* by Charles Hapgood, Elwood Babbitt had been highly psychic all of his life. At the age of five, the spirit Dr. Frederick Fisher informed the youngster of the concept of karma, which the young Babbitt readily understood. Later in his childhood, Babbitt would inform certain classmates of impending domestic violence, for example whippings awaiting them at home, which would come to pass.

In World War II Babbitt had premonitions of enemy bombings, which would come to pass shortly thereafter. Upon returning from the war, he began giving life readings in the same manner that Edgar Cayce, one of the world's most consistently accurate channels, did.

Although the main entity Babbitt channeled was Dr. Fisher, he also at various times had channeled Albert Einstein, Sam Clemens, Abraham Lincoln, and Sigmund Freud, to name a few. Amazingly, when electroencephalographs were done on Babbitt's own brain waves, those of Dr. Fisher, and on Einstein, not only were Babbitt's graphs different from Dr. Fisher's and Einstein's, but Dr. Fisher's and Einstein's were even different from each other!

Apparently, in his class on Blue Mountain in August 1987 and in private channeled readings, Babbitt and his spirit guide Dr. Fisher made a series of literally earth-shattering predictions. Among these initial predictions was a large earthquake in California and the stock market crash (to occur within a few months).

These events would be followed by massive flooding and tidal waves caused by the melting of the polar ice caps due to the ozone depletion. There also would be worldwide earthquakes, and the eruptions of Mount Vesuvius and Mount Pele would signal this catastrophic chain of events.

People were advised to be one hundred miles inland and at least 7000 feet above sea level at this time. Many who had heard these warnings were in fact making plans to vacate Southern California for mountainous regions.

I didn't know what to make of all this gloom and doom, but when the largest earthquake in 16 years rocked Southern California and a major stock market disaster occurred a scant month later, I began to reconsider this information.

I immediately read the completely enthralling *Voice of Spirit*. When I received news that the institute was bringing Mr. Babbitt to Santa Barbara for a series of classes and private readings, I promptly reserved a space for a reading. I always had wanted a trance channeled reading, but either finances or other extenuating circumstances had prevented this from happening.

One of the reasons I wanted a reading with Elwood Babbitt, or rather with his spirit guide Dr. Fisher, was that Babbitt had been channeling all of his life. He now was in his late 60s, and I wanted a trance channeled reading from someone with whom I had no previous contact. In short, I didn't want to have an excuse as rationalization for how possibly valid information may have been known.

The reading I received from Babbitt ran for about 45 minutes, and I was allowed to tape it. Since part of my aim in this book is to share what I consider to be proof that the spirit realm and reincarnation are real, I'd like to highlight just those aspects of the reading.

After he briefly explained the channeling process, which I already was quite familiar with, Babbitt closed his eyes and proceeded to go into trance. Many other channels I had experienced in group settings went into trance fairly quickly--in two or three minutes. It took Babbitt a bit longer. At one point I felt a spiraling vibration above my crown chakra, at the crown of the head. A second later Dr. Fisher abruptly began speaking rather gruffly through Babbitt.

Dr. Fisher informed me that my spirit was vibrating at 6,765,000 cycles per second. Many of my past lives were revealed to me in the discourse, but only two of them rang bells.

In one I was a senator in Pompeii named Ortarius. I was further told that wearing a golden wreath on my head and wearing robes would bring back memories of walking through hollowed hallways, and that my spirit could not stand confinement.

When I was a child, I flirted with the idea of becoming a lawyer, which was an occupation in which many legislators first begin their careers. As for the other relatable information, I've always loved open spaces. In fact, I avoided elevators at all costs.

The other life was one that took place in Germany. This was verification of what I had experienced in the gripping group regression in Verna Yater's class.

My purpose in this life, according to Dr. Fisher, could be fulfilled as a teacher of spirituality. I was told that I had the gift of clairaudience--the ability to hear what is beyond the range of the human senses. I further was told that I would be experiencing a buzzing in my ears that would occur to further this ability.

This bit of information really struck me as genuine, considering the "spirit broadcast" I had had and the little messages that came to me in rebirthing. It also was interesting that I was a musician, which obviously was related to audio, and that for the moment I made my living on the telephone! It was just too convenient for this Dr. Fisher to have known this. He could very well have stated that I had clairvoyant abilities, but this would not have been as close to the truth. Yet he did not.

I was told that as the time of these major earth changes approached, I would be living in high country and that a few years after this time I again would walk the continent of Atlantis as I once had.

Finally, and here's where I had some remaining skepticism, I was told that I would learn how to dematerialize and levitate and then teach others these fine arts as well.

When Babbitt came out of trance, he instructed me to listen to the tape over and over again and to write or call him because he always kept up with those for whom he read. I thanked him for the reading and told him I would keep in touch. I then left for home to sort things out and again listen to the tape as recommended.

I attended some workshops Elwood Babbitt gave shortly after my reading with him. The most amazing thing occurred in this workshop when Babbitt channeled what is known as the Vishnu force --the God force. Apparently this vibration is so powerful that it requires 24 spirit engineers to adjust the vibrations to make the transmission possible. One time while channeling the master force, the vibrations were so intense that it nearly blew out Babbitt's circuits and almost killed him.

Before a crowd of 60 or 70 of us on this particular day, the Vishnu force came through and caused the oddest effect. It was as if the force was a sedative. Shortly after the force came through, I was transported to some other place during most of the transmission and consequently remember very little of what had been said.

When I shared my experience with those with whom I had lunch at the break, I found that everyone had the same experience. After lunch, however, all of us were feeling alive and full of energy.

After listening to the tape that was made of that day's channeling some three or four times, I've still yet to hear or totally comprehend what had been said.

A few weeks later I had more earthquake dreams. At one point in the dream I saw a map of Australia. A few weeks later, to my surprise, a rather large earthquake did in fact hit this continent.

I went to another two-day workshop with Babbitt. More information came through Babbitt and his spirit entities concerning the earth changes. That night I had a dream.

I dreamt that I was out on the sidewalk in front of a twin movie theater and a King Cullen supermarket. These supermarkets flourished on Long Island when I was growing up, however I don't recall ever going to one.

An old man was crossing the street and approaching me. He had white hair and must have been 80 years old. He stood in front of me for a number of seconds and stared into my eyes as if I knew him. I asked him his name. We stayed in the same spots and then the scenery around us slowly faded until we were standing on a snow-covered mountain. He then replied to me that his name was Arthur.

During the break in the next day's workshop, I decided to go off by myself. Many people already were quite convinced of these earth change predictions and making their moving arrangements. Some even were selling their homes and businesses. With major quakes hitting Australia, California, Japan, and Alaska shortly after my fairly regular earthquake dreams, I wanted to be alone to think things out for myself.

I had found that there basically were two camps of metaphysical thought out there on this earth changes issue. One group held that since we create our reality by our thoughts, by putting energy into this gloom-and-doom business we would create that very thing. This made sense to me at first. Then I heard the other argument.

Yes, we did create our reality by our thoughts, and there were many people out there who were un-metaphysically minded and ruled their lives with greed and hatred. This group was sending out a lot of negative energy. This group was destroying our environment, killing off animal groups and in short raping mother earth. This negativity would be what really was responsible for the need for the earth to shed its skin. The earth needed to be cleansed. It needed a rebirth. If catastrophic disaster was the price to pay for the cleansing, so be it.

It also seemed to me that the greed group, which of course many of us have played a part in in one lifetime or other, outweighed the relatively small metaphysical group of people as a whole. Hence, the spiritually minded people who were putting stock in earth changes would not be creating this negative situation because it already existed and appeared to be getting worse.

But there was a positive aspect, a precious opportunity in the way of soul growth, which the cleansing earth changes also would bring. It has been estimated that three quarters of the earth's population would change dimensions--transpire at the time of the earth changes.

Usually when one dies, a period of rest can follow, and eventually meetings with one's guides and teachers take place. The guides and teachers help one evaluate the life just lived and assist in planning future activities in the world of spirit or in some other dimension. However, these guides do not judge.

But with so many souls entering into spirit at one time, it has been suggested that this migration would warrant the presences not only of one's guides and teachers, but also the Master Teachers: Jesus and Buddha among them.

Since many people don't believe in God or the world of spirit, they can go life after life without much soul evolution. Many even pass into spirit unwilling to accept that they have left the physical plane, as I mentioned in my out-of-body experiences chapter. So with the amount of transcendent energy available through the presence of the Masters, the possibility for quantum leaps in soul growth would exist for many of these entities.

As for those left to rebuild the Earth, there also is a possibility for soul growth. For many will come to the realization that there is a greater force than ourselves operating in the world. Through the rough times ahead, when vast amounts of cooperation will be necessary in order to rebuild, hopefully we will realize that love is the substance that connects everything together. Love is the cosmic glue of the universe, and the physical world is simply a reflection of the amount of that love or lack of it.

Since the physical world is an out-picturing of all of our thoughts and actions, hopefully we will learn to be more responsible to ourselves, one another, and the planet.

The changing times and these realizations surely will speed up the karmic process of us all. Again, there is no judgment or guilt to be attached to these events. They simply are lessons in self-realization to be learned along the way back to the Godhead.

As I went walking through the wooded area surrounding the workshop on the lunch break, I ran into a man also taking the workshop who was sitting by the creek. From what I could tell he was not a fanatical type of person.

He shared with me that he had decided to leave the area. Then he began speaking to me rather deliberately, and as if he needed to phrase what he was about to say in such a way so as not to alienate me.

"You know, Steve," he slowly began, "you and I were in a lifetime together in the days of the Knights of the Round Table."

"Hmm, that's funny," I said remembering an experience I had just a few weeks previous.

"I had this meditation in Santi's class a few weeks ago, and Merlin came to me. I was convinced that he was one of my spirit guides. What's funny is that I know nothing about that period, and always had thought that Merlin was just a myth."

Then I remembered my dream.

I attempted to put all the pieces together, then I shared my dream with this man.

"Get it? I was standing in front of a King Cullen supermarket, and then Arthur comes walking toward me. King Cullen and King Arthur."

Now I really needed some time alone.

As I was weighing all of this earth-change information, contemplating moving, and waiting for more signs that this was the right thing to do, I began seeing Colorado license plates nearly every day in my travels around Santa Barbara. I wasn't looking for them, either. My eyes would just be drawn in their direction. Then I would park my car and cars with Colorado plates would be parked right in front of me. It was starting to get to be a little too much.

One day while at work I decided to go to a nearby Mexican restaurant for lunch. I called to make sure that they had the entree I was in the mood for, since some days they were out. Such was the case on this day.

I altered my plans, and instead went to my favorite quasi-vegetarian restaurant. As I approached the restaurant I quickly remembered the health-oriented Mexican restaurant across the street (which I rarely ate at because my favorite Mexican restaurants were the authentic mom-and-pop variety). But since I was in the mood for Mexican food, I changed plans once again.

I was seated promptly, and when the chips and salsa arrived, two businessmen a table away from me began talking about Colorado Springs!

A week or so later I was talking to my mother on the phone, and she informed me that my dad had a business trip the next week in Colorado Springs! *This must be some hot spot*, I thought to myself, yet I previously never had heard of the place.

A few nights later I had another lucid dream. I was taking a Colorado license plate out of a clear plastic bag. When I woke, the dream didn't impress me one way or the other. But when I shared the dream with a friend, I flashed on the fact that in California license plates came in manila envelopes. I then remembered that the dream had been lucid. So with the clear plastic bag, and the lucidity, I reasoned that the spirit realm was attempting to make something doubly clear to me.

"Move to Colorado!"

I was quietly meditating in my bedroom one day, when suddenly I heard a bee in my ear. I immediately jumped up. I looked around for it, and not only did I not find it, I could not even hear it. This had been quite a loud buzz. I looked around for a fly, reasoning to myself that flies also buzz. But there was no fly.

There was a small garden outside my window, so I ran out to search for the bee there. But no bee was to be found. In fact, it was dead silent.

I then remembered my reading with Babbitt. Dr. Fisher had predicted that I would be hearing buzzing noises in my ears that would open me up further clairaudiently! He was accurate about the buzzing. Maybe the earth changes stories were true, too.

A new roommate moved in and was holding a garage sale one weekend to make some extra money. Not only was the sale not very well advertised, but we lived in a residential are on the outskirts of town, with little traffic. As a result of this, by one o'clock no one had shown up for the sale.

My roommate and her friend wanted to get something at the store, and so they asked me if I would watch the sale for a few minutes. I consented, and five minutes after they left a car pulled up. In fact, it was the only car that would show up for the entire day. Of course, it had a Colorado plate on it! When I asked the woman where in Colorado she had moved from, she said Colorado Springs.

I quickly gave her a summary of my experiences as of late. When I told her of my lucid Colorado license plate dream, she commented, "But in Colorado, the license plates *do* come in plastic bags."

Maybe these were the signs I was waiting for, and I would be moving to Colorado after all.

I had just seen a terrifically depressing film, Woody Allen's *September*. Perhaps the film just mirrored depressing aspects of my own life back to me. Three people in the film were in unrequited love with other people, and in addition each of the participants still was trying to figure out what to do with their lives.

I went to the late show, which I usually avoid because I get sleepy. But when the movie was over, instead of being tired I found myself thoroughly confused and depressed. I sat in my car and talked aloud to myself.

This process was not a foreign one to me, as I usually wrote songs this way. The rhythm of the road created a beat, and I would sing against the beat, finding melodies and riffs along the way. But now I was desperate, and if it would be a song that I was writing, it was one that hit too close to home to sing just now.

I questioned my motives for leaving Santa Barbara to move to Colorado. I thought about the possibility of going back to school. I questioned leaving a more-than-decent paying job, although it was one that I did not particularly like, for a different, more intuitive adventure.

My voice eventually fell into meter. I then started my car, continuing this poetic channeling of my higher and lower selves, and proceeded home.

Halfway home, I moved the verse to music, and I now was singing my stream of consciousness dirge. As I approached my street around midnight, I stopped this desperate song of my soul to the night and the voices started in my head.

What am I doing?

I started questioning all of my metaphysical beliefs and all that had happened along the way.

What am I, deep end material? I thought to myself.

And why did I recommend that stupid piece on UFOs to Nancy? I recently had read an article that suggested the possibility of alleged UFO encounters being synonymous with some kind of initiation rite.

I sat talking aloud to myself across the street from my house for some time. As I questioned my recommendation of this UFO article to Nancy, something dramatic occurred.

Halfway down the street the sky lit up in front of me, an explosive Polaroid flash in the night. For a second I was an animated negative. Then a silvery object shot through the dead black sky and across the universe.

I intuitively followed the light through my side window.

A shooting star, I quickly rationalized to myself. But then remembering the explosion of light I had just witnessed, I realized this was no shooting star. It was something else, too. It was another incident of synchronicity from on high, another clue to consider in my overall perceptions of things.

Maybe I soon would be moving to the mountains.

I ran into the house to tell my roommates of this freak incident. Santi, who now was one of my roommates, was the only one who really believed me. We ran back outside to look for any remaining traces, but met a starry black sky instead.

A passerby was making his way down the street at this late hour.

"Did you see that?" I anxiously questioned him.

"Yeah, I did."

I suddenly found myself hugging this total stranger since we immediately were cosmic comrades.

"What was that?" I pleaded.

"Well, gee, ya know, at first I thought it was like a shooting star or something...."

"So did I!" I interrupted.

"But it must have been...," he began as we both stopped and looked at each other with the full knowledge that we had just had a close encounter of the first kind, "...a UFO, I guess."

When I wrote about this incident later in my journal, I knew it was another sign that it was time for me to move. I could no longer ignore what I was receiving. I also knew that when we follow our intuition, we come closer to God and our God Selves, our Higher

Selves, and closer to fulfilling that for which we have come again.

The next day I called the media and the police to report my sighting and to see if there had been any other reports. Nothing. At least I had a witness in the passerby I had encountered (or rather accosted) after the experience.

I further investigated to see if perhaps nearby Vandenberg Air Force Base had launched any test missiles, as they do from time to time, which would have been visible from Santa Barbara. Again there was nothing. So with my pragmatic left brain satisfied, I chose to believe that this was indeed a UFO that we had witnessed and that it was also another sign for me.

With all of the signs I had received pointing me in the direction of Colorado, I finally decided that I *would* move. I gave notice at my place of employment, a cellular phone company.

I got along very well with my manager. After I shared my news with him, he informed me that he had received a promotion and also would be leaving the area.

The new manager began training while I finished out the month. I didn't pay too much attention to him, but apparently others did. After he officially assumed his new role, the head of installations quit. A clerical person quickly followed. Then one of the top salespeople put in for a transfer. It was not a pretty scene. I looked at my perfectly orchestrated departure from this toxic environment as the final go-ahead from the Universe.

Chapter 30

Daniel

Shortly after this time, I went for a bike ride early one evening to watch the sunset by the beach. Even though I had made my decision to move, I still was living with the uncertainties. So the ride was a perfect vehicle, in more ways than one, for this type of reflection.

I loved the long shadows of the palm trees that I found waiting for me on the grassy parks that ran along the bike path by the beach. There was something very comforting to me about the shadow play that occurred at dusk--especially here.

I locked my bike and went down to the beach to watch the sun's final embers. To me this was as peaceful as the world could be. The rhythmic, reassuring sound of the lapping waves, the cool evening breeze, the shadows on the cold sand beneath my feet were very soothing.

But now the coolness, combined with my increasing hunger, interrupted my reverie, so I quickly scooted back to the grass and palm trees that now were disguised as shadows against the Maxfield Parrish blue night sky. I hopped on my bike and headed up the street.

There were a number of other cyclists out, and I took my time because it was getting dark and I couldn't see very well. One of the people I spotted looked vaguely familiar to me, but I couldn't place him. I pedaled slowly, still transfixed from my meditative sunset ritual. As I got closer to the other cyclist, he spoke first.

After sharing greetings, we remembered that we had taken a class together at University of California at Santa Barbara. He was an attorney now. I realized that fourteen years had passed, along with so much angst, since our class. We rode together slowly, reminiscing and laughing about being older. Then he asked what I was doing.

I went into my musical and theatrical accomplishments. I briefly told him how I made my living. Then I opened up a can of worms.

"And I'm moving in a few weeks to Colorado."

"What's going on out there?" he asked.

I didn't know where to begin, or if I even would attempt it.

"Oh, you know, change of pace. I've been here for a while and I've been in kind of a slump. I don't know," I stalled.

It would take so long to explain why I was moving. There was so much to tell and I didn't know where he was metaphysically or spiritually. I really didn't want further scrutiny after all of my soul searching. So I began cautiously.

"I've been depressed for a while over a relationship--or rather a nonrelationship."

This was true, in fact I usually needed to physically remove myself from an area where such a devastating depression had occurred.

He empathized with my situation.

From that moment on I felt that I could trust him. So I quickly plunged into earth changes and so on. Surprisingly, he was quite intrigued.

I found myself going back to my earlier experiences to give him some kind of perspective on my madness, or perhaps to validate my new plans for myself.

"Hey, have you eaten?" he interjected at one point, "I'm starved; I haven't eaten all day."

We agreed on a nearby casual eatery and pedaled off.

I did most of the talking, as I remember it. I talked about my spirit broadcast, about many of my dream state experiences, rebirthing, and the other reasons I was now leaving paradise for the unknown.

"This stuff's great!" he exclaimed at one point, and without a hint of sarcasm in his voice.

"Have you written any of this down? It would make a great book."

I told him that I had started a few years ago but didn't think I had enough material, and went through the "Who am I to write a book?" conversation.

"I'd read it," he returned.

I told him of my tarot card readings regarding writing a book, but again, I think mainly to convince myself. I continued to feel out the idea as we talked.

We finished our meal and biked slowly back to town. When we reached his house, we continued our rambling conversation. I was getting tired, and I'm sure he was, too, so we said our good-byes, swapped addresses, and I sped home.

It was so dark that night that I felt like I was swimming through all of the memories I had just shared as I cruised across town. I felt a renewed sense of conviction in what I was doing with my life. But writing the book still remained a tentative abstraction.

Chapter 31

The Whole Thing's a Vortex

I had hoped to find a traveling companion with whom to share my drive to Colorado. Even though I had decided on the move, with the help of the continual messages, I still had some fear. It mostly was fear of the unknown. This was another reason I had sought someone to travel with.

As my departure date approached, I had exhausted all of my possibilities for a traveling partner and resigned myself to making the trek alone.

But surprisingly, after a little work on myself, I felt good about the situation and was no longer so fearful. In fact, I felt empowered by having gone through another wall of fear that proved imaginary.

Unfortunately, however, a bookkeeping problem at work delayed procurement of my final paycheck, causing me to delay my trip for almost a week. I had to improvise a little and stay with friends. But I felt put out considering how antsy I was to get on the road.

I was having lunch at a restaurant with friends one day when a pair of unidentified hands suddenly cupped my eyes from behind me, leaving me in the dark. There was nothing mystical about the experience, as in my rebirthing incident with the sensation of hands on my hands. It was just a friend I hadn't seen in a while being a wise guy.

He joined my other friends and I at the table, and then I told him of my upcoming journey.

"Hey, do you want to come along for the ride?" I asked jokingly.

To my surprise he didn't take it as a joke. In fact, when I outlined the route and the number of days I planned to be on the road, he began to seriously consider joining me in the adventure.

The next day Charles called with the news that he would travel with me to the Rocky Mountain state. I was happy to have the company, and it would make the trip more fun. Now I really was excited to leave. I explained my predicament regarding having to wait for my paycheck, and Charles was as flexible about it as I had been forced to become.

In retrospect I again noticed how angry I had become over having to delay my trip instead of trusting. The delay had given me a chance to work on my fear of traveling alone and also allowed a traveling companion to manifest once the fear had been conquered.

There also was another benefit I received in allowing the universe to plot the next chain of events for me. I was able to take the company to the labor board for their negligence in paying me promptly since I had given more than adequate notice. It would take a few months of red tape, but I finally was compensated nicely for the inconvenience.

One of the things about spirituality/metaphysics that always seemed true for me was that the rules the universe played by actually were quite simple. Yet regardless of how simple a concept such as trust could be, I always needed to be reminded of the rules. But if I could get what I wanted (a traveling companion) and a little extra cash, it was all right if the universe slapped my wrists, or rather my ego, once in a while.

We finally hit the rode and opted for the southern route. We decided to stretch the trip to three days, taking the extra time to explore a bit.

The first night we slept in Flagstaff, Arizona, or rather "Flagtown" as Charles kept referring to it. I always had imagined Flagstaff to be a big town for some reason, and so I was quite surprised to find what looked like a deserted logging community.

The next day we journeyed into Sedona, one of the "energy vortex" capitals of the world. These high-energy locales were said to heighten one's awareness. They could trigger past-life recall and amplify spirit communication. They also amplified one's healing abilities and one's energies in general.

Something had gotten amplified, for up until then Charles and I had a more than pleasant trip. Now we were at each other's throats and lashing out at each other with our new age technology, in response to the intense energy we now were encountering.

We finally mellowed out and actually started laughing. Talk about releasing! We went into Boynton Canyon, where one of the main vortexes lies. In the middle of the loop of a road that we were on, we stopped and asked a security guard at some country club which way the vortex was.

"The whole thing's a vortex!" he comically exclaimed.

I liked that. My new look on life, *The Whole Thing's a Vortex*! *You fool! Why hadn't you seen it before?* It was so obvious. I liked it. It was a nice, succinct little concept.

Since we already were in the vortex, we drove a while and then got out of the car to hike around. I went off by myself and meditated for a while. I won't say that it was exactly peaceful. It probably took one some time to get used to the vibrations. But nonetheless I achieved a pleasant feeling of elevation in my meditation.

However, I had an eerie feeling the next day as we neared Sante Fe. It was a feeling of both mystery and desertion. Upon arriving in the city, the feelings didn't go away. It was like the whole town was in on something that I wasn't.

Since I had heard that Sante Fe was a very spiritual place, the effect that the town was now having on me was doubly baffling. I felt like a real outsider. So did Charles.

We were anxious to get to Colorado Springs, or "the Springs" as it is called. After a quiet lunch of New Mexican cuisine, we briefly browsed the shops and then hit the road for our final destination.

It was nightfall as we proceeded to get lost on the final five-mile leg of our tour. We already were in the Springs and now were look-ing for Manitou Springs, where I would be camping out at my friend Lois's house.

When we finally arrived, we found the house filled with other friends also taking refuge at Lois's while acclimating to the area and house hunting. I felt like I was home.

The next day the group had planned a trip up to Blue Mountain. The workshop and camping center needed to be cleaned up from the winter's ravaging paws before classes could begin, and there was a lot of work to be done.

The mountain was another high-energy vortex like Sedona. Ac-cording to the information retrieved from spirit, the mountain would be one of the twelve safe citadels in North America at the time of the earth changes, housing thousands of people at a time.

In previous summers there had been claims of UFO sightings, as well as visitations from Jesus and other Masters at Blue Mountain. Chief Tukawa, said to be the guardian of the land, also was reported to have made appearances from time to time.

With these psychic manifestations, the high energy of the land, and the work done in the transformational workshops facilitated by Verna Yater and others, more and more people were experiencing profound breakthroughs in their lives while at Blue Mountain.

Naturally, I was quite excited now to finally have my peak "experience," hopefully of this sacred place. Sedona, Sante Fe, and now Blue Mountain, I certainly was getting a good share of "juice" these last few days.

More than anything else, I noticed a sense of peace, tranquility, and stillness as I walked the land and surveyed the vistas. It clearly was a paradise. As for the psychic stories, so far I had not seen any Indians or saints--at least not yet. But I had to admit the vibrations did feel good.

I stayed with Lois and company only a few days, as I was anxious to get settled and have my own space again. Charles flew back to California and I began looking for a new home.

Colorado Springs did little for me, but the surrounding mountainous regions, like Manitou Springs, nestled just below majestic Pike's Peak, were stunningly beautiful. After spending just a few days in Manitou, I knew that this was where I would live.

I had lived in a similar setting when I still was in college in northern California's Stanislaus County, living fifty miles from the back gate of Yosemite National Park in Mark Twain country.

Now in Manitou, a tiny little mountain town that depended on summer tourism to survive, I walked the winding, hilly streets and jotted down phone numbers from the many "for rent" signs I spotted along the way.

I met a young woman who worked as a clerk at a nearby imported clothing shop one day. She was very friendly. The next day I spotted her on the street with a man who, judging by the quality of their embrace, was more than likely her lover.

The following day, while being shown a prospective apartment, I spotted the young man again. This time he was walking up the stairs to the side of the unit I was being shown.

He said hello as he continued sprinting up the narrow steps.

The apartment was very charming in a funky kind of way. It was the bottom half of a duplex built up on a little hill. The wonderful French windows that lined the front of the living room faced the street. There also was a front door that led to a small deck. Across the street was a stream flowing beneath lush trees.

I already had decided to take the place when the future landlady informed me that her parents lived in Santa Barbara. This only solidified my decision. Later, while moving in, I discovered that the young woman and her boyfriend were my upstairs neighbors. So the clues were continuing.

Chapter 32

Future Visions

" Live the day as if it were here."
--Friedrich Nietzsche

My next step was to find some work. I had spent quite a bit of my savings traveling and now securing the new apartment. Most of my transplanted California friends were doing volunteer work for the institute on the mountain for the summer. I felt a little left out, but I needed to make some money.

In a conversation with Verna, I let it be known that I also would like to help support the institute, too, but I would need to be compensated. There was a paying position open in enrollment for that summer's classes on the mountain, so I immediately took it. It was a way of supporting myself and the institute and being a part of things all at the same time.

I always had done some form of sales job even though it was not the occupation of my choice. But my economic state and the lack of other interesting positions seemed to necessitate this form of employment from time to time. This was one of those times.

But this time it would be different because the work was related to spiritual growth and possibly could be fulfilling. I needed to be doing something fulfilling in order to be able to throw myself into any work.

I got to travel around quite a bit, mostly north to Denver and Boulder, to promote the mountain and Verna's work. I booked Verna on radio and television and organized "Evenings with Spirit," as they were billed, in which Verna would trance channel and do healing work in group settings. On these evenings I would introduce Verna, speak about the upcoming workshops, and talk about the mountain to the group. These evenings usually were uplifting and lively events largely due to the healing energies that Verna channeled.

The more challenging aspect of my new job, however, was the

actual enrollment process. This process entailed speaking with people on the phone who had previously experienced Verna and the work of the institute.

I then would find out what people were looking for in their lives-- what was missing and where the blocks were. This was where the job could get prickly. Some people found talking about their lives help- ful, and even if they did not enroll in a class, they received clarity through talking with me about their direction and their next step. Others were more secretive and did not wish to participate. Many of these people were deathly afraid. There were those who could not talk about what it was they were afraid of, or even admit to having fears, yet for some reason they also would not hang up the phone, either.

However, when people did talk, things came up. I certainly was not a trained therapist, but I did know resistance when I saw it. I had experienced many lives worth in rebirthing alone!

While I was not a therapist, I did know what would occur in many of the different workshops that were being offered. The process that I was using was designed to find out what people were looking for so that I then could recommend a workshop to them. I could lead them to a workshop for the type of experience they desired, or help those with unclear inner problems and blocks by recommending workshops that were catalytic in nature and potentially could help bring them out of themselves and into contact with what they needed to work on or needed to be healed.

Many of the people I coached were where I had been four or five years earlier, not knowing which book to read next and wanting spiritual experiences and direction. They were very new to it all. I found more and more that I was recommending books and sharing some of my experiences with people who wanted to hear more. The more I shared with people, the more open and receptive they became. I could feel shifts taking place, and in some instances real break- throughs.

Whether or not these people enrolled in classes was not so impor- tant to me. Ideally, I would have liked everyone with whom I spoke to have attended a class, because based on what I was hearing, there was a lot of pain out there. I knew how much they would benefit from the experience. But the fact that I could reach people, share my knowledge, and make even a little difference was very fulfilling and made what I was doing rewarding for me.

It also was frustrating at many times, for even after some people who needed healing had decided to come to a workshop, their fear and resistance were so great that they subconsciously would create obstacles at the last minute that prevented them from attending. Cars broke down. Baby-sitters suddenly were unavailable. It was the same scenario that happened to many on their fourth or fifth session in rebirthing.

I had experienced so much fear and resistance in rebirthing that I easily could relate to it. But I also knew the rewards I reaped by trusting and going through wall after wall of fear.

It got to the point where one welcomed these challenges with open arms. In fact, many of my friends and I were in this category. We were eager to dump whatever remaining junk was in the way of our accomplishing all that we had come in this life to do. In this often painful growth process, we were courageous. They inspired me. We inspired one another. It was a contagious kind of courage.

In my travels around town one day, I came upon a twin movie theatre that resembled the location from the dream with Arthur. I looked around for a supermarket but found none. Maybe I just wanted it to be there as a sign of confirmation.

But when I turned the corner and went back off the road, I did find a supermarket. It wasn't a King Cullen, however, but it was a King Soopers!

That was enough of a confirmation for me. When I thought about it, though, it may very well have been a King Soopers in my dream and I identified it or remembered it as a King Cullen because this was my only point of reference. It was amazing to me how spirit could have retrieved something so buried in the recesses of my mind so that I would remember the dream and now have the knowingness that I had moved to the right place.

The first weekend of summer classes on the mountain arrived, and Jill Jarrett (my Santa Barbara counterpart in enrollment and friend who had worked with Santi in rebirthing) and I decided to take the workshop. The majority of classes and workshops I had taken over the years had been facilitated by Verna and were oriented toward psychic development. I had done dream work, past-life work, guided meditations to meet my guides, psychometry, and an intensive channeling workshop with Verna. But the sort of workshop Verna was doing on the mountain this summer was one that I had not previously experienced with her.

The workshop had to do with vision. The focus was geared toward finding out what one's vision was and what was blocking the vision, and then how to get committed to that vision in order to bring it into fruition.

I had wanted to experience this workshop so that I could tell people firsthand what the mountain experience was like. Many people simply were afraid of the unknown, as I had been at times in the course of my many journeys. If I could share what they might expect in these breakthrough-oriented workshops, the accommodations, and my experiences in general, I would be of better service.

Since my depression I had been on automatic, and outside of following my intuition to move to Colorado, I wasn't doing much with my life. Since this was the case, it was funny that it hadn't occurred to me to fully participate in the workshop. Maybe this was my way of resisting.

At any rate, I thought I would stay in the background and simply observe. But it didn't turn out that way.

Early on in the workshop, I watched others become vulnerable; open up; share their stories; and experience pain through fear, anger, and/or tears. I saw remarkable healing take place. I knew what I had received from the humbling and harrowing rebirthing experience, so I was not going to let the opportunity to release more junk that I was carrying around with me slip by now.

We sat in a circle in the event tent with the sides rolled up, which offered a magnificent panoramic view of the nearby mountains thick with pines and firs of every species. An Indian talking stick was passed around to whomever wished to speak. When I reached for the stick, I shared with the group that I knew I had lots of anger bottled up inside of me that needed release. Now I felt funny because while I knew this anger still was inside of me, I now was feeling light and playful in these wondrous surroundings and with these beautiful, supportive beings of love.

I sat in the center of the circle in a chair. Behind another chair facing me, Verna began to go into some role playing with me. Since I was in a pretty good space, I couldn't feel to the depth where I knew the rage lay boiling. Since I had done a fair amount of acting, I felt like I almost was performing. Then a shift occurred. Verna had hit on something, and I got angry!

Immediately, I started violently attacking the chair facing me with the wooden club while screaming every expletive known to man in rapid succession. With whack after whack, pieces of the thick wooden bat flew through the tent in all directions. Finally, I was holding only air.

Another stick was quickly thrown to me. Now in my rage, I jumped up and began attacking the center pole of the tent with my pent-up fury. More chunks of wood went airborne. The wood now was cutting into my hand, only I didn't feel it.

I whacked the post repeatedly and screamed obscenities until my vocal chords were raw and I had no breath left. With the last gasp I collapsed onto the chair behind me, and unexpectedly began sobbing profusely.

I immediately knew that my anger had been a mask for my tears. While in my tirade I had been lashing out at everyone who ever had hurt me, it was for myself and the love that I didn't always feel and desperately needed to feel that I cried.

When I totally was back in my body, I could feel the pain in my hand, which was now bleeding, from my violent display with the rough-barked club. One by one, each member of the group supported me with loving hugs. I could feel what they had experienced through what I had done for myself. I could feel their joys and pains. All of us were in this together. That was how this workshop worked. As each person opened up, it became safer and safer to share with the group. Even if you did not share anything, you still could relate to what was going on and release in a more private way.

Shortly after my release, we broke for lunch. I could feel major shifts taking place inside of me and wanted to be by myself. I participated in the rest of the workshop but kept a low profile.

Later in the workshop, after we had the opportunity to release some of our excess baggage, we began focusing on vision. Verna led the discussion by sharing her vision for Blue Mountain with us. Her vision was quite grandiose.

Verna envisioned a sound and color complex on the land for personal healing and consciousness raising. There would be a pyramid structure that would serve to draw energies from the earth, and an amplification chamber below the glass flooring that would contain powerful crystals to further charge this energy. This structure would hold up to 80 people at one time.

A sacred receiving building would be constructed and act as a focal point to draw in energies from other planetary dimensions. This temple-like structure would also be used for ceremony. In addition, broadcast facilities for satellite uplink were also part of Verna's plan.

Of course, there would be space made available for participant housing. In all of this construction, utmost attention would be paid to the land so as to disturb it as little as possible.

Verna's vision also included serving as a catalyst for the building of other light centers and for connecting them. In addition to the 12 centers in North America, other centers would spring up in the Pyrenees, Africa, and Australia. Talk about a vision!

In addition to getting rid of the garbage that kept us stuck in our lives, I learned that it wasn't enough just to have a vision. It wasn't even enough to have a plan mapped out to ensure success. What one needed to do was to get committed to the vision.

So many of us lived our lives out of our circumstances. But to achieve a vision, great or small, this type of thinking just would not do. In order to achieve one's vision, it was necessary to get committed to the vision by making the vision the center of one's life and placing the other aspects of one's life around it. This usually required a huge shift for many, because most people lived just to survive. In fact, the idea of a vision was beyond the grasp of many people. In some instances it actually was a threat.

While in such a supportive environment, and in the presence of someone as inspiring as Verna, I began re-evaluating what I was doing with my life. What was my vision?

While the work that I was doing for the institute was important and fulfilling, it also was frustrating. It wasn't what I really loved doing. What did I love doing? What could I contribute to the world to affect positive change and balance karma? What was my vision?

The mountain was the perfect place for reflection whether or not one was taking a workshop there. In fact, in addition to the classes on the mountain, the institute also offered what they called "transitional days," custom-made private retreats.

In my reflection I thought about conversations I had with people, like my college friend, Daniel, who had little or no orientation to the different spiritual/ metaphysical concepts and experiences available. I thought about what I had experienced while doing enrollment and while acting as a spokesperson from time to time for the institute. When I thought about these things, I realized that everyone I spoke with had varied spiritual experiences, had read different books, and were at different stages of their spiritual unfoldments. I discovered that there were those consciously (as well as unconsciously) on their spiritual paths.

Laying dappled by the sun in a wide rope hammock, I breathed in the intoxicating, fresh, musky, pine-scented air and began thinking of all that had happened to me since I had embarked on my spiritual adventure. I thought about rebirthing, the intense depression I endured, working with my dreams, my precognitive dreams, the lucid dreams, astrology, the UFO incident, and all of the signs that had pointed me to Colorado.

Then I began thinking of all that had happened to me when I first began to unfold. I thought about the spirit broadcast, the out-of-body episodes, the past-life experiences, my ring changing color overnight, and all of those early weeks of inexplicable synchronicity when I landed the job at the computer accessories company.

I also thought about the two tarot card readings I had received regarding a book that I would write. I thought about my false start in writing it, and I thought about a message from spirit that I received once in meditation.

For some reason a cloud had popped into my mind's eye. Inside the cloud was the face of a classmate from grammar school. I had not been friends with him and had not seen him since we had graduated. His name was Stephen Wright. The subtle message from spirit said, "Stephen, write!"

I thought about my conversation with Daniel. When I thought about all that had happened in the three of four years since I first sat down to write, I realized that I had learned a great deal, had witnessed some amazing things, and unexpectedly had experienced profound changes in my life. Now I did have a book inside of me.

When I finally began writing, the book poured forth effortlessly. It all happened so fast, I felt myself being pulled toward destiny. I felt a little like Dorothy in *The Wizard of Oz* in that I probably could have written the book at any time. But like Dorothy on her journey to Oz, I needed to go through my process of discovery, too.

Epilogue

The Harvest

"For everything there is a season."
--Ecclesiastes 3:1

The cataclysmic earth changes have not yet happened, but it is said that the rhythmic patterns of time that spirit employs do not always coincide directly with our time frame. With the "greenhouse effect" heating up the planet, we already are experiencing earth changes. Is the much-prophesied cataclysm still in the cards, and if so, is it reversible? I don't know.

As for moving to Colorado, the work that I've done with others through the institute and the work I have done on myself there is positive proof to me that it was a move I was meant to make.

Shirley MacLaine's *Out on a Limb* opened me up to possibilities and my search. My path. You may be intrigued enough to go back later and read that book as well.

However, I maintain that since I now know there are no such things as coincidences that that book was a catalyst for me at a time when I was ripe for the experiences I subsequently had. Since everyone is different, their experiences will differ, too. A book may make one aware of one's path, or it could be an experience. The experience could be as deliberate as taking a psychic or spiritual development class or as spontaneous as a psychic experience in or out of the dream state.

In retrospect I find this strange, because at the time these "things" started happening to me--seemingly from out of the blue--I was convinced that everyone needed to read MacLaine's book and that that was the only way they, too, could have similar experiences. I also felt it was the only way they could have known I had not gone crazy.

I'm still learning, exploring, and growing. I know we are here to know and love ourselves and then to know and love God, as the

210 From Out of the Blue

spirit entity Indira Latari so often reminds us. The information and experiences I've presented in this book have been of help to me in my unraveling process.

It can be a challenge for one to remember one's purpose, and it is easy to lose sight of it even when gained. Plateau periods through the course of one's spiritual journey realistically can be expected.

I have discovered that part of my purpose is to disseminate spiritual knowledge, as the spirit teacher Dr. Fisher had verified. In reexperiencing all that had happened to me in the writing of this book, I've been able to appreciate again for myself the gifts I had been given and share these gifts with others.

My adventure in consciousness began in the fall of one year and I completed the writing of this book a few autumns later--"coincidentally" at the time of the harvest. It was September.

Appendix A

Bejeweled Book Meditation

Began with a prayer of thanks and protection. For example: "I ask that only the greatest, and the highest, and the best, be present with me just here and just now, and that all other conditions and circumstances be removed. For this opportunity I give great thanks."

Then sit up straight in a chair or on the floor with your legs uncrossed. Turn palms up or down on your lap.

Now close your eyes and picture a book before you. This is your special book. On the cover of this golden book are dazzling jewels. There can be glittering emeralds, rubies, and diamonds.

Now take a moment to design your special book. You can use your favorite gems or crystals or whatever you wish. But really *see* it.

When you're ready, slowly open your book to the first page. See an inkwell holding an exquisite quill pen. Color the ink any color you wish. See your hand take the pen from its well. Dip the pen once and you will have all the ink you will need. Now take your hand to the top left page and write your name the way you refer to yourself.

When you have finished, go to the top of the right page and write the words "deep trance." Now go back and forth, writing your name on one page and "deep trance" on the other. If you are not comfortable writing with the pen, experiment with what works best for you (write on slippery wax paper, try finger paints, or write with a ballpoint pen). Get as creative as you like, until you are comfortable with your writing method.

When you are through meditating slowly and gently bring yourself back to your book. Place your pen back in its well and then close the book. Put it back on its shelf or wherever you would like to keep it. Know that whenever you would like to, you may return to it.

Appendix B

Working with Dreams

Remembering Dreams

The first step in working with dreams is being able to remember them. The best way to remember one's dreams is to set an intention to do so before drifting into sleep. This plants a potent seed in the subconscious.

It also is advisable to have either a pad, pen, or a tape recorder accessible by one's bedside, along with a dim lamp. Upon waking in the middle of the night, one usually can remember one's last dream. Being careful to keep movement to a minimum, begin jotting down the dreams. It especially is important to write down dreams that are so powerful that they wake us, as these dreams usually hold many clues and messages.

Before getting out of bed in the morning, more dreams can be added to the list. I've found it helpful to re-read the dreams from the middle of the night, because in so doing I usually remember more dreams and details that I had missed writing down previously.

Working with Dreams

There are many ways of working with dreams. In one method, begin by reliving the dream on paper, writing with as much detail as possible. Include your feelings at each changing interval in the dream.

Next, comprise a list of all of the symbols. Go back over the list and pick out the three or four most important symbols. A good way to test the importance of a symbol is to close your eyes and feel the symbol. The symbols with the most charge--the symbols that press a button in us--usually are the ones with which to work.

After you have your symbols, write down the first symbol on the top of a sheet of paper divided into two columns below the symbol. (I usually keep a spiral notebook exclusively for working with dreams so I can date the dreams and refer back to them.)

For the rest of the exercise, you either can work with a partner or by yourself. Working with a partner initially is beneficial because it gives you the opportunity to freely associate more easily, which is crucial to the exercise. Later, after you've become more adept in working with your dreams, you can get good results by working alone.

If you're working with a partner, pick a specific dream and then the first symbol from your list of symbols from that dream. Have your partner then rapidly ask you *repeatedly* what you like about the symbol. Stick with your first impressions. Associate freely rather than think through your responses. You will have many.

As you respond, your partner will transcribe your responses in the first column. Work quickly, and don't be afraid to repeat a response if it keeps coming up. It is undoubtedly an important clue. You should work for at least five minutes per symbol. You'll be surprised at how much information you'll gather.

When you've exhausted what you liked about the symbol, repeat the procedure with what you did not like about the symbol. Your partner then will enter these responses in the remaining column.

After you've finished the first symbol, do the remaining two or three symbols from the dream on which you are working. Only work on one dream at a time or you'll get confused.

When you've finished with your likes and dislikes of each symbol, your partner then will read back to you what you liked about the symbol. From this list pick the one response that you resonated to most, and have your partner circle it. Repeat this procedure with the most striking dislike of the symbol (again have your partner circle the response). Do this for the remaining symbols.

When you are finished, list the symbols with the circled responses on a separate sheet of paper. In so doing you probably will begin to see some correlations and gain some clarity about the dream.

Frequently, when I've done two or more dreams from the same chosen night, with two or three symbols from each dream, I see that the message that I got was the same in all of my dreams for that night. But experiment for yourself.

If one of the symbols still puzzles you, take a clean sheet of paper and draw the symbol on the entire sheet. If you want to get creative with crayons, inks, paint, or another media, feel free to do so. This may bring you closer to understanding the significance of the symbol.

While holding the sheet of paper with the symbol in front of your face like a mask, become the symbol. To assist you in this, have your partner ask you--as the symbol--a series of questions beginning with who, what, when, where, or how. Your partner can ask anything of you, with the exception of a "why" question. For example, if the symbol were a door, your partner should ask, "What does it feel like to be a door?" "Where do you live, door?" "When were you born, door?" Your partner will record your replies.

This new information and experience, coupled with the previous exercise, usually is quite effective in unravelling dreams. The more you work creatively with dreams, the more able you will be to see which dreams were symbolic, past-life flashes, meetings with your guides, or other possible experiences. You will strengthen your relationship with your guides and teachers and gain enormous self-clarity.

As I've mentioned earlier in this text, the awake state is as much of a dream as the dreams we dream in our sleep. Since this is the case, the little episodes that weave together to form the fabric of our lives can be viewed as dreams also, complete with symbols.

Since these experiences are dreams, we can work with the symbols that appear in our everyday lives in the previously mentioned ways as well. For example, if we get a flat tire, this becomes a symbol we may want to consider working on.

This concept of being able to work on symbols in our awake state as if they were sleep state dream symbols is further reinforced by synchronicity, the theory that states there are no accidents or coincidences.

Lucid Dreaming

There were many different methods outlined in the LaBerge book for achieving the lucid state in the dream state. I like what seemed to me to be the most simple and one of LaBerge's personal methods.

To begin with, it is helpful to set an intention at some point in the day to have a lucid dream that night and to remind yourself of this intention throughout the course of the day. Before closing your eyes for the night, the next step is to again reaffirm the intention to have a lucid dream. While still awake but with eyes closed, repeat, "One, I'm dreaming, two, I'm dreaming..." (and so on) to yourself until dreaming occurs.

If you are lucky enough to enter into a lucid dream at this point--due to technicalities having to do with rapid eye movement (REM)--the lucidity probably will not last for very long.

In the course of the night, however, possibly between 3 and 5 A.M., the same procedure of counting "One, I'm dreaming..." should be repeated upon awaking. My experience has been that with the repetition of this phrase at this time of night, lucidity in the dream state results almost immediately and can be extended for quite a long period of time.

LaBerge further mentions that from his personal experience, naps in the late afternoon provide a climate for lucid dreaming six times greater than at night.

Appendix C

Affirmations

Affirmations are positive statements describing what we want to bring into our lives. Affirmations can be used to cultivate a lacking attribute in ourselves, (for example, "I am an infinitely loving person"). Maybe the affirmation will be used to bring material objects one's way ("Endless money is flowing to me **now**!") or to rid ourselves of unwanted, undeserved emotions. For instance, if one was feeling guilty about something but knows all the while that he is innocent, the affirmation might be "I am totally innocent of any wrongdoings."

Affirmations also can be employed to bring any sort of relationship into one's life ("I now have a meaningful, growth-oriented relationship with the partner of my divine selection").

The possibilities for affirmations is endless. However, the necessary ingredients of an affirmation are always phrasing the affirmation in the present and always using a positive expression. For instance, if one was feeling like a failure, he would not phrase the affirmation "I am no longer a failure." Instead, a possibility could be "I now am extremely successful in everything I do." One does not necessarily have to believe the affirmation in order to work with it.

Here are some simple ways to work with affirmations. It's best to work with only two or three affirmations at a time. You can work with them either by writing them down or by recording them on a tape deck. Pick your first affirmation. Make sure it is set in the present and that all of the words are positive. Be as specific as possible. However, try to keep one's options open. For instance, if you are working with an employment affirmation, you can mention a specific job opportunity that you are interested in, but simply add "...or the job that will serve my highest good."

Generality is best in relationships as well ("I now have a multitude of loving and supportive friends who accept me" or "I now have a loving, growth-oriented partnership with the mate of my divine selection").

If you are writing down your affirmations on paper, write them 20 times two or three times a day. Writing them in the morning helps set the mood for the day. Writing them just before bed plants some potent positive seeds into the highly programmable subconscious.

When you begin writing the first affirmation and doubts pop up, as they tend to, acknowledge the doubt by writing down your feelings toward the affirmation on the line beneath the affirmation. All of us are complex people with many mixed voices inside of us. It helps to both integrate the voice and bring the affirmation into fruition by honoring these voices when they speak to us.

After you have written down the doubtful, negative, and possibly angry voice responses, continue writing your affirmation until you've written it 20 times. Then go to the other affirmations with which you plan to work.

A method I get good results with when working with a tape recorder is to record each affirmation ten to 20 times. Play the tape at least two or three times a day and repeat the affirmation along with the tape. When your doubts come up, stop the tape and speak them. Then play the affirmation until your doubts subside.

I like this method because I often am in my car and can listen to my affirmations frequently. It also helps keep my mind off of the traffic. Sometimes I even make up little melodies to go along with the affirmation and then sing them. This I feel really helps lodge new positive ideas into the subconscious.

Whichever method you use, repeat these procedures for ten consecutive days per affirmation. When you've completed a ten-day interval, you can pick new affirmations or continue with some with which you currently are working. Then let them go.

If, after a few months, you still have not achieved the desired condition or situation, you may want to return to that affirmation. You may find that you had denied some of your feelings or doubts and that this got in the way of manifesting.

One last word on affirmations. Keep your affirmations to yourself! Sometimes people--friends, family, or loved ones--don't understand affirmations or believe that they work. This unnecessary negativity can be a strain and counterproductive to your good intentions. So only share your affirmations with those you know will support you.

For more information on affirmations, I highly recommend *I Deserve Love* by Sondra Ray, and Florence Scovel Shinn's inspirational *The Game of Life and How to Play It*.

Bibliography

Affirmations

Jim Leonard and Phil Lout, *Rebirthing: The Science of Enjoying All of Your Life*, Trinity Press, 1983.
Sondra Ray, *I Deserve Love*, Les Femmes, 1976.
Florence Scovel Shinn, *The Game of Life and How to Play It*, DeVorss and Company, 1925.

Astrology

Stephen Arroyo, *Astrology, Karma, and Transformation*, CRCS Publications, 1978.
Stephen Arroyo, *Astrology, Psychology, and the Four Elements*, CRCS Publications, 1975.
Jeff Green, *Pluto: The Evolutionary Journey of the Soul*, Llewellyn Publications, 1986.
Liz Greene, *Relating: An Astrological Guide to Living with Others on a Small Planet*, Samuel Weiser, Inc., 1978.
Liz Greene, *Saturn: A New Look at an Old Devil*, Samuel Weiser, Inc., 1978.
Robert Hand, *Planets in Transit*, Para Research Inc., 1976.
Grant Lewi, *Heaven Knows What*, Llewellyn Publications, 1967.
Martin Schulman, *Karmic Astrology, The Moon's Nodes and Reincarnation*, vol. 1, Samuel Weiser, Inc., 1975.

Channeling

Leah Garfield and Jack Grant, *Companions in Spirit*, Celestial Arts, 1984.
Charles H. Hapgood, *Talks with Christ and His Teachers Through the Psychic Gifts of Elwood Babbitt*, Fine Line Books, 1981.
Charles Hapgood, *Voices of Spirit Through the Psychic Experiences of*

Elwood Babbitt, Fine Line Books, 1975.
Ruth Montgomery, *A Search for the Truth*, Fawcett Crest/ Ballantine Books, 1966.
Jane Roberts, *Seth Material*, Bantam Books, 1976.
Jane Roberts, *Seth Speaks*, Bantam Books, 1974.
Sanaya Roman and Duane Packer, *Opening to Channel*, H.J. Kramer Inc., 1987.

Healing

Mary Greer, *Tarot for Yourself*, Newcastle Publishing, 1984.
Louise Hay, *You Can Heal Your Life*, Hay House, 1982.
Dr. W. Brugh Joy, *Joy's Way*, J.P. Tarcher, Inc., 1979.
Shirley MacLaine, *Going Within*, Bantam Books, 1989.
Dr. Scott Peck, *The Road Less Traveled*, Simon and Schuster, 1978.
Florence Scovel Shinn, *The Game of Life and How to Play It*, DeVorss and Company, 1925.
Dr. Frances Vaughan, *The Inward Arc*, New Science Library, 1986.

Inspirational Reading

Richard Bach, *Illusions: The Adventures of a Reluctant Messiah*, Dell Publishing, 1977.
Thaddeus Golas, *The Lazy Man's Guide to Enlightenment*, Bantam Books, 1980.
Nora Grafton, *My True Psychic Adventures*, Tolff Publishers, 1977.
Dr. Gerald G. Jampolsky, *Love Is Letting Go of Fear*, Bantam Books, 1981.
Ken Keyes, Jr., *The Handbook to Higher Consciousness*, Love Line Books, 1975.
Shirley MacLaine, *It's All in the Playing*, Bantam Books, 1987.
Shirley MacLaine, *Out on a Limb*, Bantam Books, 1983.
Og Mandino, *The Greatest Salesman in the World*, Bantam Books, 1974.
Richard Millman, *The Way of the Peaceful Warrior*, H.J. Kramer Inc., 1984.
Kit Tremaine, *The Butterfly Rises*, Blue Dolphin Publishing, 1987.

Intuition

Dr. Frances E. Vaughan, *Awakening Intuition*, Anchor Books, 1979.

Lucid Dreaming

Stephen LaBerge, *Lucid Dreaming*, Ballantine Books, 1985.

Manifesting (see **Prosperity**)

Out-of-Body Travel

Robert A. Monroe, *Journeys Out of the Body*, Doubleday and Co. Inc., 1977.

Prosperity

Shakti Gawain, *Creative Visualization*, Bantam Books, 1982.
Jerry Gilles, *Moneylove*, Warner Books, 1978.
John Randolph Price, *The Superbeings*, Quartus Books, 1981.
Sondra Ray, *I Deserve Love*, Les Femmes, 1976.
Jane Roberts, *Seth Speaks*, Bantam Books, 1974.
Frances Scovel Shinn, *The Game of Life and How to Play It*, DeVorss and Company, 1925.

Rebirthing

Leonard Or and Sondra Ray, *Rebirthing in the New Age*, Celestial Arts, 1977.
Jim Leonard and Phil Lout, *Rebirthing: The Science of Enjoying the Rest of Your Life*, Trinity Press, 1983.

Reincarnation

S.L. Cranston and Joseph Head, *Reincarnation*, Causeways Books, 1967.
Edith Fiore, *You've Been Here Before*, Coward, McCann, and Geoghegan, 1978.
Shirley MacLaine, *Dancing in the Light*, Bantam Books, 1985.
Dr. Helen Wambach, *Life Before Life*, Bantam Books, 1979.
Dr. Helen Wambach, *Reliving Past Lives*, Harper and Row, Publishers Inc., 1978.

Tarot

Alfred Douglas, *The Tarot*, Penguin Books, 1973.
Mary Greer, *Tarot for Yourself*, Newcastle Publishing, 1984.